# Stamp Collecting for Beginners: From Hobbyist to Expert

Avi Meir Zaslavsky, Dmytro Yurikov, Lucas Martin

**Disclaimer**

This book is designed to provide educational and informational insights into the fascinating world of stamp collecting. While every effort has been made to ensure the accuracy and completeness of the information contained herein, neither the author nor the publisher can guarantee its applicability to your circumstances.

Stamp collecting, like any other hobby or investment, carries certain risks. So, you are encouraged to research and seek professional advice before making significant purchases or investments.

The opinions expressed in this book are those of the author and do not necessarily reflect the views of any organizations or institutions mentioned. They are not responsible for any liability, loss, or damage incurred directly or indirectly from using the information in this book.

The book's content, including any financial or market data, historical references, and personal opinions, is subject to change without notice. The inclusion of any specific products, services, or companies does not imply endorsement or recommendation by the author or publisher.

By reading this book, you agree to indemnify and hold harmless the author and publisher from all claims, liabilities, damages, or expenses arising from your use or reliance on the information provided.

# Contents

| | |
|---|---|
| Introduction | 1 |
| Chapter 1: The History and Evolution of Stamp Collecting | 4 |
| Chapter 2: Getting Started: Essential Tools and Supplies You Need | 23 |
| Chapter 3: The Different Types of Stamps | 39 |
| Chapter 4: Building Your Collection: Where to Find Stamps | 54 |
| Chapter 5: How to Evaluate and Identify Stamps | 66 |
| Chapter 6: Organizing Your Collection | 82 |
| Chapter 7: How to Preserve and Maintain Your Stamps | 97 |
| Chapter 8: Specializing Your Collection | 111 |
| Chapter 9: The Art of Trading and Selling Stamps | 126 |
| Chapter 10: Attend Stamp Shows and Exhibitions | 141 |
| Chapter 11: Understanding Stamp Catalogs | 153 |
| Chapter 12: Stamp Collecting as an Investment | 168 |
| Chapter 13: My Top Secrets for Finding Rare Stamps | 183 |
| Chapter 14: Advanced Collecting Techniques | 195 |

Chapter 15: Future Trends in Stamp Collecting      208

Conclusion      220

# Introduction

My journey into stamp collecting began quite unexpectedly. It was a rainy afternoon, and I stumbled upon an old box in my grandmother's attic. Among the trinkets and memorabilia, I found a dusty album filled with stamps from various countries. This was the spark that ignited my passion for stamp collecting.

As I went deeper into the world of philately, my collection has grown from a modest album to a vast treasure trove of stamps from around the globe. From common postage stamps to rare finds, every addition to my collection had a unique story.

I have also attended stamp shows, joined philatelic societies, and connected with fellow enthusiasts, each interaction enriching my knowledge and collection.

Stamp collecting is more than just a hobby; it's a journey through history and a connection to the world. This book aims to share the joy and fulfillment that comes from building and curating a stamp collection.

In this book, you'll find comprehensive information on all aspects of stamp collecting. We'll start with the basics, such as understanding different types of stamps and essential tools for beginners.

As we progress, I'll share advanced techniques for identifying, valuing, and preserving stamps. You'll also learn how to find rare stamps, build a specialized collection, and even consider stamp collecting as an investment.

Each chapter is designed to provide practical advice and insights, making your journey into stamp collecting enjoyable and rewarding.

# Chapter 1: The History and Evolution of Stamp Collecting

W hen it comes to any hobby or venture, it's essential to understand the history behind it. Every activity, no matter how small or seemingly insignificant, has a rich history that shapes its principles and practices.

Without this understanding, it's easy to get lost in the chaos and lack the value that comes with knowing where you're coming from. Stamp collecting, also known as philately, is no exception. As we delve into the world of collecting stamps, it's crucial to first explore the history and evolution of this fascinating hobby.

The history of stamp collecting dates back to the mid-19th century, when the first postage stamps were introduced. As the world became more interconnected through trade and communication, the need for standardized postage systems arose.

This led to the creation of the first postage stamps, which were initially used to facilitate international mail. Over time, the design and production of stamps evolved, reflecting the cultural, social, and economic changes of the time. Today, stamp collecting is a global phenomenon, with millions of enthusiasts worldwide.

Understanding the history of stamp collecting is vital because it provides context and meaning to the activity. Without knowing how and why stamps were created, it's difficult to appreciate their significance and the stories they tell.

The history of stamp collecting is a testament to human innovation, creativity, and the power of communication. By learning about the evolution of stamps, we gain a deeper appreciation for the art, design, and cultural significance of these small pieces of paper.

## The Birth of Postage Stamps

The story of postage stamps began in the early 19th century. Back then, sending a letter was a complicated and often expensive process.

STAMP COLLECTING FOR BEGINNERS: FROM... 7

The cost was usually based on the distance the letter traveled and the number of sheets of paper it contained.

What's more, the recipient, not the sender, typically paid for the delivery. This system caused all sorts of problems, including undelivered mail when people refused to pay.

Sir Rowland Hill, a British schoolteacher and social reformer, believed the postal system needed a complete overhaul. In 1837, he published a pamphlet called "Post Office Reform: Its Importance and Practicability," which proposed several radical ideas.

One of his key suggestions was the introduction of a pre-paid adhesive postage stamp, a small piece of paper that could be affixed to a letter to show prepayment of postage.

Hill's idea was revolutionary. By 1840, his proposal had become a reality with the introduction of the world's first postage stamp, the Penny Black. This small, black stamp featured a profile of Queen Victoria and was sold for one penny.

For the first time, the cost of mailing a letter was the same regardless of distance within the United Kingdom. It was a simple yet effective solution that changed postal systems forever.

The Penny Black was an immediate success. People loved the convenience of being able to prepay for their mail. It wasn't long before other countries adopted similar systems.

Brazil issued its first stamps in 1843, known as the Bull's Eyes, and the United States followed suit in 1847 with stamps featuring Benjamin Franklin and George Washington.

What made these early stamps so fascinating wasn't just their practical use but also their designs. The images and artwork on stamps often reflected a country's culture, history, and values. Collectors soon began to see stamps as miniature works of art and valuable pieces of history, not just postage.

The success of the Penny Black also set off a wave of postal reforms worldwide. It streamlined the mailing process, made it more reliable, and significantly boosted communication.

For the first time, people could easily and affordably send letters across great distances, fostering better connections between friends, family, and businesses.

So, the birth of postage stamps marked more than just a change in how mail was paid for. It represented a shift towards a more accessible and efficient communication system.

It's fascinating to think how a small piece of paper could have such a profound impact on the world and make it easier for people to stay connected.

## Early Stamp Collectors and Their Stories

Stamp collecting has a rich history. One of the earliest known stamp collectors was John Edward Gray, a British zoologist. In 1840, when the first postage stamp, the Penny Black, was issued, Gray immediately saw its potential.

He wasn't just interested in the stamp's utility; he was captivated by its design and the idea of collecting these miniature works of art. Gray's early efforts laid the groundwork for what would become a global hobby.

Then there was the story of a young French woman, Mademoiselle Hortense. She began collecting stamps in the 1840s, soon after they were first introduced.

Her collection started with stamps she found on letters sent to her family. Hortense meticulously removed the stamps from envelopes, carefully preserving them in a scrapbook. Her passion for collecting spread through her social circles, sparking interest among her friends and family.

In the United States, one of the first notable stamp collectors was Charles Lathrop Pack. Pack was an American businessman with a keen interest in stamps. He began collecting in the mid-19th century and quickly amassed an impressive collection.

Pack's dedication to stamp collecting was so intense that he became a founding member of the American Philatelic Society in 1886. His efforts helped popularize stamp collecting in America and set high standards for future collectors.

Another fascinating figure was Philipp von Ferrary, an Austrian nobleman who lived in the late 19th and early 20th centuries. Ferrary's collection was legendary, comprising some of the rarest and most valuable stamps in the world.

He was known to travel extensively, purchasing entire collections from other collectors and dealers. Ferrary's passion for stamps was unmatched, and his collection became the envy of collectors worldwide. His dedication showed that stamp collecting wasn't just a hobby; it could be a serious pursuit.

Moving to the 20th century, we have Alfred F. Lichtenstein, an American lawyer and philanthropist. Lichtenstein started collecting stamps as a child and never lost his enthusiasm. He specialized in British Commonwealth stamps, and his collection was known for its depth and quality.

Lichtenstein's approach to stamp collecting was meticulous, and he became a respected figure in the philatelic community. His collection, which he generously shared with others, inspired many to take up the hobby.

One of the more unusual stories is that of Princess Grace of Monaco. Yes, the Hollywood actress turned princess was an avid stamp collector. Grace Kelly developed an interest in stamps as a child and continued collecting throughout her life.

Her collection focused on stamps from Monaco and featured many unique pieces. Princess Grace's involvement in stamp collecting added a touch of glamor to the hobby and showed that collectors come from all walks of life.

Finally, there's the story of Count Philipp von Ferrari. Despite his aristocratic background, Ferrari was a humble and passionate collector. He owned some of the rarest stamps, including the famous "Treskilling Yellow," a misprinted Swedish stamp that is one of the most valuable in the world.

Ferrari's collection was so vast and valuable that after his death, it was sold off in a series of auctions that captivated the philatelic world. His story is a testament to the enduring appeal of stamp collecting and the lengths to which collectors will go to build their collections.

## Major Milestones in Stamp History

Stamp collecting has a rich history full of fascinating milestones. One of the earliest and most significant events was the introduction of the world's first postage stamp, the Penny Black, in 1840. Issued by the United Kingdom, the Penny Black featured a profile of Queen Victoria.

As stamp collecting gained popularity, so did the diversity of stamps. By the mid-19th century, many countries had started issuing their own stamps.

In 1847, the United States released its first stamps featuring Benjamin Franklin and George Washington. These early stamps are highly sought after by collectors today, not only for their historical significance but also for their designs.

Another milestone came in 1856 when British Guiana issued the famous 1c magenta stamp. This stamp is unique because only one copy is known to exist. It has changed hands multiple times, fetching millions of dollars at auctions.

The story of the 1c magenta adds an element of mystery and excitement to the world of stamp collecting, showing how a small piece of paper can become a valuable treasure.

The late 19th and early 20th centuries saw the rise of commemorative stamps. These stamps were issued to celebrate significant events, people, and anniversaries.

For example, in 1893, the United States issued the Columbian Exposition stamps to commemorate the 400th anniversary of Christopher Columbus's voyage to the Americas. These stamps were colorful, and detailed, and became instant favorites among collectors.

The 20th century also introduced airmail stamps, which marked the beginning of a new era in postal history. In 1918, the United States released the first airmail stamp featuring a picture of a Curtiss Jenny airplane.

Interestingly, a printing error resulted in a few stamps with the airplane printed upside down, known as the "Inverted Jenny." These error stamps are incredibly rare and highly prized by collectors.

The world of stamp collecting continued to evolve with the advent of thematic or topical stamps in the mid-20th century. These stamps focused on specific themes, such as animals, sports, or famous people, appealing to a broader audience.

Collectors could now build specialized collections based on their personal interests, making stamp collecting more diverse and engaging.

In recent years, the digital age has brought about new milestones in stamp collecting. Online platforms and digital catalogs have made it easier for collectors to buy, sell, and trade stamps globally.

Virtual stamp exhibitions and digital albums have also emerged, allowing collectors to showcase their collections to a wider audience.

These modern advancements have ensured that stamp collecting remains a vibrant and dynamic hobby.

## **Stamp Collecting in the 21st Century**

Stamp collecting has come a long way from its humble beginnings. Today, it's a vibrant and dynamic hobby that attracts people of all ages and backgrounds.

With the advent of the internet and digital tools, the way we collect, trade, and learn about stamps has changed dramatically. Gone are the days when collectors had to rely solely on local dealers or physical catalogs. Now, a world of stamps is just a click away.

One of the biggest changes in modern stamp collecting is the rise of online marketplaces. Websites like eBay, Delcampe, and various specialized auction sites have made it easier than ever to find and purchase stamps from around the world.

These platforms offer a vast array of stamps, from common issues to rare and valuable pieces. Collectors can browse listings, compare prices, and even bid on auctions from the comfort of their own homes.

Social media has also had a huge impact on the stamp collecting community. Platforms like Facebook, Instagram, and specialized forums allow collectors to connect, share their collections, and exchange tips and advice.

There are countless groups and pages dedicated to stamp collecting, where members can post photos of their latest finds, ask questions, and engage in lively discussions. It's a fantastic way to meet fellow enthusiasts and stay up-to-date with the latest trends in the hobby.

# STAMP COLLECTING FOR BEGINNERS: FROM... 21

Another exciting development in the modern stamp collecting landscape is the growing interest in thematic and topical collections. Collectors today are not just focusing on traditional country-based collections; they are also exploring themes like animals, space exploration, historical events, and more.

This shift has opened up new avenues for creativity and personalization in stamp collecting. It's fascinating to see how stamps can tell stories and reflect personal interests.

Stamp shows and exhibitions remain an important part of the hobby, but they too have evolved. Many shows now offer virtual components, allowing collectors who can't attend in person to participate online.

These virtual shows often include live auctions, virtual tours of exhibits, and online dealer booths. It's a great way to experience the excitement of a stamp show without leaving your home.

Lastly, the modern stamp collecting landscape is characterized by a strong sense of community and camaraderie. Despite the digital shift, the core values of sharing, learning, and connecting with others remain at the heart of the hobby.

Whether you're a seasoned collector or just starting out, there's always someone willing to offer advice, share stories, and celebrate the joy of stamp collecting with you. It's this sense of belonging that continues to make stamp collecting a beloved and enduring pastime.

# Chapter 2: Getting Started: Essential Tools and Supplies You Need

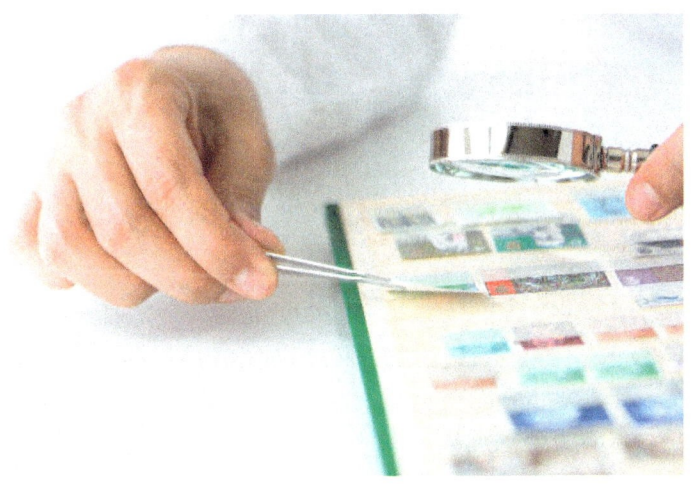

As a stamp collector, you know that the journey from casual enthusiast to dedicated collector requires more than just a passion for philately. To truly excel in this hobby, you need the right tools and supplies to help you organize, preserve, and showcase your collection.

The right tools and supplies are essential for any serious stamp collector. They help you to efficiently manage your collection, ensuring that each stamp is properly stored, handled, and displayed.

With the right equipment, you can easily identify and categorize your stamps, making it easier to find specific stamps and track your progress. Moreover, the right tools help you to preserve your stamps, protecting them from damage and ensuring that they remain in excellent condition for years to come.

Without these tools and supplies, you may find yourself struggling to keep up with your growing collection, or worse, risking damage to your precious stamps.

## Getting Started: Essential Tools and Supplies

When you're starting out with stamp collecting, having the right tools can make a world of difference. Trust me, investing in a few basic items will save you a lot of frustration and help you enjoy your new hobby even more. Let's talk about the must-have tools for every beginner stamp collector.

First on the list is a good pair of stamp tongs. These are special tweezers designed to handle stamps gently without damaging them. Regular tweezers can be too harsh and might leave marks or tears.

Stamp tongs have smooth, flat tips that make it easy to pick up and move stamps around without harming them. You'll find that they come in various shapes and sizes, but a simple pair with rounded tips is perfect to start with.

The next tool you need is a magnifying glass. Stamps are small and often have intricate details that are hard to see with the naked eye. A magnifying glass helps you appreciate the fine artwork and spot any tiny flaws or marks that could affect a stamp's value.

You don't need anything too fancy—a basic handheld magnifier will do the trick. Some collectors also like to use magnifiers with built-in lights for better visibility.

Stamp albums are another essential. This is where you'll store and display your collection. Albums come in different styles and sizes, but for beginners, a simple stock book or a ring binder with clear plastic pages works great.

These albums protect your stamps from dust, moisture, and damage, while also allowing you to organize them neatly. To keep your stamps safe, you'll also need stamp mounts.

Most collectors use stamp hinges — which are small and gummed pieces of paper that help you attach stamps to album pages. While they are easy to use, they also leave a mark on the back of the stamp.

If you want to keep your stamps in pristine condition, consider using stamp mounts instead. These are clear, plastic holders that protect both sides of the stamp and can be attached to album pages without adhesive.

A perforation gauge is another handy tool for identifying stamps. Stamps have tiny holes along their edges, called perforations, which help in separating them from a sheet. The number and spacing of these perforations can be used to identify different stamps. A perforation gauge is a simple tool that measures these holes, helping you determine the exact type of stamp you have.

Lastly, a good reference book or stamp catalog is invaluable. These books contain pictures and information about a wide variety of stamps, helping you identify and value your collection.

They also provide fascinating background stories and historical context for many stamps. Having a reliable reference guide will enhance your understanding and appreciation of the stamps you collect.

With these basic tools in your toolkit, you're well on your way to becoming a successful stamp collector. Remember, it's all about enjoying the process and discovering the fascinating world of stamps. Happy collecting!

## Understanding Stamp Albums and Storage Options

Stamp albums are important for any good stamp collection. Think of them as the home for your stamps, where each one can be displayed and admired.

There are stockbooks, hingeless albums, and traditional stamp albums, each with its pros and cons. The key is to find one that suits your needs and makes organizing your collection a joy rather than a chore.

Stockbooks are a fantastic option for beginners. They have plastic or glassine strips on each page where you can easily slide your stamps in and out. No adhesives, no mess.

This is great because you can rearrange your collection as it grows without damaging any stamps. I remember the thrill of my first stockbook, flipping through the pages, each filled with colorful stamps from all over the world.

Hingeless albums are another excellent choice, especially if you're looking to keep your stamps in mint condition. These albums have pre-mounted transparent pockets, so you don't need to use stamp hinges or mounts.

Your stamps stay pristine, and you get to enjoy a clear view of both the front and back of each stamp. It's like giving each stamp its own little showcase.

Traditional stamp albums, on the other hand, require a bit more hands-on effort. You use stamp hinges or mounts to affix your stamps to the pages. This can be a bit tricky at first, but it's a rewarding process.

It feels like you're crafting a personal scrapbook of history. Plus, many traditional albums come with printed spaces and information about each stamp, which can be quite educational.

When choosing an album, consider the type of stamps you collect. If you're into thematic collecting, like stamps featuring birds or famous historical figures, an album with customizable pages might be best.

You can create sections for each theme, making it easier to find and admire your favorites. This personalized approach adds a fun and unique touch to your collection.

Storage options don't end with albums, though. You'll need a safe place to keep your albums, away from direct sunlight, humidity, and pests. A cool, dry place is ideal. I've found that a sturdy bookshelf works wonders. Just make sure the albums are upright and not crammed together, as this can cause the pages to warp over time.

## Cleaning and Handling Your Stamps

When it comes to cleaning and handling your stamps, there are a few basics you need to know. First off, always handle your stamps with clean hands or, better yet, use stamp tongs.

These little tools help you avoid getting oils and dirt from your fingers on the stamps, which can cause damage over time. Trust me, you don't want a fingerprint smudge on that rare find you just added to your collection.

Now, let's talk about cleaning. Stamps are delicate, so you need to be gentle. If you have a stamp that's a bit dirty, never use water or harsh chemicals. Instead, try a dry cleaning pad or a stamp eraser.

STAMP COLLECTING FOR BEGINNERS: FROM...    33

Stamp erasers are specially made for stamps and can help remove dirt without causing harm. Just gently rub the stamp in a circular motion, and you'll be amazed at how much cleaner it looks.

For those stubborn spots, like old adhesive or gum residue, you might need something a bit stronger. One trick is to use a little bit of talcum powder or cornstarch. Lightly dust the back of the stamp and then gently rub it off with a soft brush. This can help lift off the sticky residue without damaging the stamp itself.

When it comes to removing stamps from envelopes, be extra careful. Soaking stamps is a common method, but it can be tricky. Use lukewarm water and let the stamp float off the paper.

Never peel it off, as this can tear the stamp or damage the perforations. After soaking, let the stamp dry on a clean surface, like a blotting paper, and gently press it with a flat object to keep it from curling.

Another tip is to always store your stamps properly after handling or cleaning them. Keep them in a cool, dry place away from direct sunlight. Humidity and heat can cause stamps to curl, fade, or even mold. Using protective sleeves or mounts can also help keep your stamps in pristine condition.

Remember, the goal is to preserve the integrity and value of your stamps. Handling and cleaning them with care ensures they remain beautiful and valuable for years to come. Plus, there's something incredibly satisfying about looking at a clean, well-preserved stamp that you've taken the time to care for properly.

### Setting Up Your Workspace

Creating the perfect workspace for stamp collecting is essential for enjoying the hobby and keeping your collection in top condition. You don't need a lot of space, but you do need a clean, well-organized area where you can comfortably work on your collection.

First, find a spot in your home that can be dedicated to your stamp activities. It doesn't have to be a whole room; a corner of a quiet room or a small desk can work just fine.

The key is to have a place where you can leave your tools and collection out without them getting disturbed. Avoid high-traffic areas where your stamps might get accidentally damaged.

Lighting is crucial in your workspace. Good lighting helps you see the details on your stamps and spot any imperfections. Natural light is the best, so setting up near a window is ideal.

If that's not possible, invest in a good desk lamp with an adjustable arm and a bright, white light bulb. This will help reduce eye strain and make it easier to work for extended periods.

Your workspace should also be free from dust and moisture. Stamps are delicate and can be easily damaged by dirt and humidity. Use a clean, dry cloth to wipe down your workspace regularly. If you live in a humid area, consider using a dehumidifier to keep the air dry. This will help preserve your stamps and prevent any mold or mildew from forming.

Organization is another key factor. Keep your tools, such as tweezers, magnifying glass, and perforation gauge, within easy reach. Use small containers or drawers to store these tools neatly.

A clutter-free workspace not only makes it easier to find what you need but also helps keep your stamps safe. When everything has its place, you can focus more on enjoying your collection.

It's also a good idea to have a comfortable chair. You might spend hours sorting through stamps, so having a chair that supports your back can make a big difference.

Consider getting a chair with adjustable height and good lumbar support. Your comfort matters because it allows you to enjoy your hobby without any physical discomfort.

Finally, personalize your space. Add some personal touches like a favorite picture, a small plant, or even a framed stamp from your collection.

This will make your workspace inviting and inspire you to spend more time there. Remember, this is your special area for indulging in your passion, so make it a place you love to be in.

# Chapter 3: The Different Types of Stamps

As a stamp collector, it's important to have a solid understanding of the different types of stamps available. Stamps come in a wide variety of shapes, sizes, designs, and materials, each with its own unique history and significance.

Knowing the differences between these stamp types can help you better appreciate the art and culture behind each piece, as well as make more informed decisions when building your collection.

## Definitive vs. Commemorative Stamps

When you start collecting stamps, one of the first things you'll notice is that not all stamps are the same. Some are used every day and seem pretty common, while others are special and often more colorful or detailed.

These two types of stamps are known as definitive and commemorative stamps. Understanding the difference between them is key to becoming a savvy stamp collector.

Definitive stamps are used by the postal system. They are issued in large quantities and are used for everyday mail. You've probably seen these on your letters and packages.

They often feature designs that stay the same for years, such as national symbols, famous people, or simple patterns. Because they are printed in huge numbers and used regularly, definitive stamps are generally easy to find and less expensive to collect.

On the other hand, commemorative stamps are like the limited edition prints of the stamp world. These stamps are issued to celebrate or honor a specific event, person, place, or theme.

For example, you might find commemorative stamps for a country's independence day, the Olympics, or the anniversary of a famous person's birth. They are usually more colorful and elaborate than definitive stamps and are only available for a short period.

The designs of commemorative stamps are often unique and artistic, making them highly appealing to collectors. Since they are not printed in as large quantities as definitive stamps, they can be harder to find, especially years after their release. This rarity makes commemorative stamps more valuable over time, which is one reason why collectors love them.

When you first start your collection, you might find yourself naturally drawn to commemorative stamps because of their vibrant designs and special themes. However, don't overlook the charm and historical significance of definitive stamps.

Collecting both types can give you a well-rounded and interesting collection. Plus, definitive stamps can sometimes come with variations, like different watermarks or perforations, adding another layer of interest.

A great way to enhance your collection is to focus on a mix of both definitive and commemorative stamps from different periods and countries. This approach not only diversifies your collection but also gives you a broader understanding of the history and culture behind the stamps.

So, as you dive into the world of stamp collecting, remember that both definitive and commemorative stamps have their own unique appeal and value. Enjoy the hunt for these little pieces and let your collection grow in both variety and significance.

### Rare and Valuable Stamps

Rare and valuable stamps are the jewels of any stamp collection. These stamps are not just old or unique; they carry stories and histories that make them incredibly special.

Collecting them can be both thrilling and rewarding. Imagine holding a tiny piece of history in your hands, something that has traveled through time and places, seen by few and owned by even fewer.

One of the most famous rare stamps is the British Guiana 1c Magenta, often called the world's most valuable stamp. It's a small, scrappy piece of paper that has fetched millions at auctions.

Its rarity comes from the fact that only one exists in the world. The stamp was issued in 1856, and over the years, it has passed through many hands, each owner adding a piece to its fascinating story.

Another well-known rarity is the Penny Black, which was the world's first adhesive postage stamp. Although it's not as rare as some other stamps, its historical significance makes it highly valuable.

The Penny Black was issued in 1840 in the United Kingdom and features a profile of Queen Victoria. It's a favorite among collectors not only for its age but also for its place in postal history.

The Inverted Jenny is another stamp that many collectors dream of owning. Issued in the United States in 1918, this stamp shows a picture of an airplane printed upside down. Only 100 of these error stamps are known to exist, making it a prized possession. The story of how these stamps came to be and how they were discovered adds to their allure and value.

Stamps from small countries or territories can also be rare and valuable. For instance, the Hawaiian Missionaries are some of the most sought-after stamps by collectors. These stamps were issued by the Kingdom of Hawaii before it became a part of the United States.

They are called "Missionaries" because they were primarily used by missionaries in the 1850s. Their scarcity and historical background make them highly desirable.

Errors and misprints can make a stamp rare and valuable too. The Basel Dove is a prime example of this. Issued in Switzerland in 1845, it features a beautiful design of a dove carrying a letter.

Some copies of this stamp have printing errors, such as misaligned colors, which significantly increase their value. Collectors love these quirks because they tell a unique story about the printing process and the times in which the stamps were made.

Condition is crucial when it comes to the value of rare stamps. A stamp in mint condition, meaning it has never been used and is as fresh as the day it was printed, is worth much more than a used one.

However, even used stamps can be valuable if they are rare enough. Factors like the stamp's centering, color, and any damage or imperfections all play a role in determining its value.

## Thematic and Topical Collections

Thematic and topical stamp collections are all about focusing on a specific subject or theme. Unlike traditional collections, which might center around a particular country or era, thematic collections bring together stamps from all over the world that share a common theme.

Whether it's animals, sports, historical events, or even famous people, the possibilities are endless. This type of collecting can be incredibly rewarding because it allows you to dive deep into a subject you're passionate about.

One of the best things about thematic collecting is that it's very personal. You get to choose a theme that excites you. For instance, if you love butterflies, you can build a collection featuring butterfly stamps from different countries and time periods. This not only makes your collection unique but also keeps you engaged and motivated to find new additions.

Starting a thematic collection is pretty straightforward. Begin by choosing a theme that interests you. Then, start looking for stamps that fit within that theme.

You can find these stamps through various channels such as online marketplaces, stamp shows, or even by trading with other collectors. Remember, the goal is to have fun and learn more about your chosen theme as you go along.

Thematic collections can also be educational. As you gather stamps, you'll likely find yourself learning more about the subject you've chosen. For example, if you're collecting stamps related to space exploration, you'll come across stamps commemorating significant events like the moon landing or the launch of the Hubble Space Telescope. This adds an extra layer of depth and enjoyment to your hobby.

### Local vs. International Stamps

When it comes to stamp collecting, one of the first distinctions you'll encounter is between local and international stamps. Local stamps are those issued by your own country.

They're often the easiest to start with because they're readily available at your local post office, from local dealers, or even in your daily mail. These stamps are a great way to get familiar with the basics of stamp collecting without venturing too far from home.

International stamps, on the other hand, come from countries all around the world. Collecting these can be a thrilling adventure, offering a glimpse into the culture, history, and art of different nations.

Each country's stamps reflect its unique identity, featuring national heroes, significant events, natural wonders, and cultural symbols. This variety adds a rich diversity to your collection, making it more interesting and visually appealing.

One of the most exciting aspects of collecting international stamps is the challenge of finding them. Unlike local stamps, which you can easily purchase or receive in the mail, international stamps often require more effort to obtain.

You might find them through international dealers, online marketplaces, or by trading with collectors from other countries. This adds a fun element of discovery and connection to your hobby.

In addition to the thrill of the hunt, collecting international stamps can also broaden your horizons. You'll learn about different countries and their histories, gaining a better understanding of the world.

It's like having a miniature global tour right in your stamp album. Plus, it can be a great conversation starter when you share your collection with others.

On the practical side, there are some differences in how local and international stamps are used and valued. Local stamps are usually more common and, therefore, might be less valuable individually.

However, rare or special edition local stamps can still hold significant value. International stamps, especially those from countries with smaller postal services or limited print runs, can sometimes be more valuable due to their rarity.

When you start collecting international stamps, it's important to familiarize yourself with the various postal systems and stamp catalogs. Each country has its own way of issuing and cataloging stamps, which can affect their value and how they're collected. There are plenty of resources and guides available to help you navigate this aspect of the hobby.

Ultimately, whether you choose to focus on local or international stamps, or a mix of both, is entirely up to you. Each approach has its own rewards and challenges.

The key is to enjoy the process and let your curiosity guide you. Stamp collecting is a hobby that can grow and evolve with you, providing endless opportunities for learning and discovery.

# Chapter 4: Building Your Collection: Where to Find Stamps

When I first started collecting stamps, I was overwhelmed by the sheer number of options available. I had no idea where to begin, and I found myself wandering aimlessly through thrift stores, antique shops, and online marketplaces, searching for that elusive rare stamp. It was frustrating, to say the least. I would often leave empty-handed, feeling like I had wasted my time and energy.

I can only imagine how new collectors must feel when they're starting out. The thought of scouring the globe for the perfect stamp can be daunting, especially when you're not sure where to look. I remember feeling like I was the only one who didn't know what they were doing, and that everyone else seemed to have a secret stash of stamps hidden away.

But the truth is, finding stamps is a process, and it takes time and patience. In this chapter, I'll be sharing my own experiences and the strategies I used to build my collection.

From scouring local thrift stores to digging through online marketplaces, I'll be taking you on a journey through the world of stamp collecting. I'll share my tips and tricks for finding the best stamps, and how to navigate the sometimes confusing world of stamp collecting.

## Local and Online Stamp Dealers

Finding stamps from local and online dealers is one of the best ways to start building your collection. When I first started collecting, local dealers were my primary source.

There's something special about walking into a shop filled with stamps from all over the world. The thrill of flipping through albums and discovering hidden gems was incredibly exciting.

One of the first challenges I faced was locating reputable local dealers. Not every city has a stamp shop, so it took some research. I asked around at local libraries and community centers and found a couple of shops in nearby towns.

Visiting these dealers required some travel, but it was worth it. I remember my first trip to a local dealer; the shop owner was a seasoned collector and offered valuable advice.

Building a relationship with local dealers can be very rewarding. They often have vast knowledge and can help you find specific stamps or offer insights into your collection.

My local dealer became a mentor of sorts, guiding me through the intricacies of stamp collecting. He introduced me to other collectors and invited me to join local philatelic clubs. These connections were invaluable in expanding my collection and knowledge.

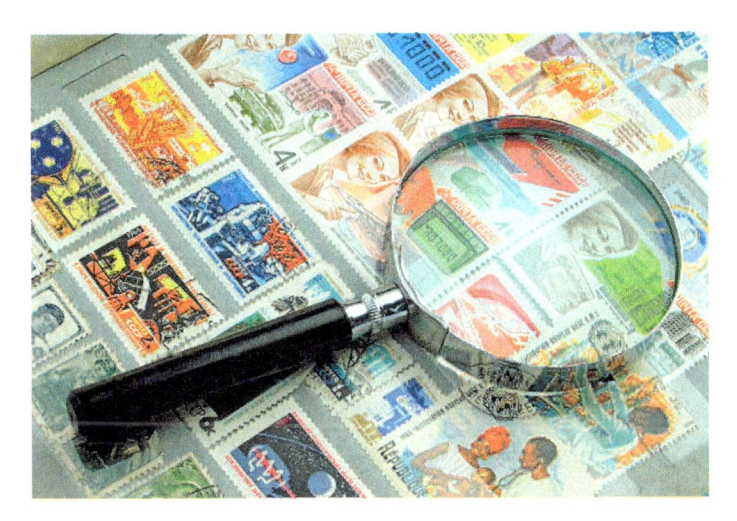

However, there were also challenges. Prices at local dealers can sometimes be higher, and the selection might be limited compared to online options. I remember feeling frustrated when I couldn't find certain stamps I wanted.

But I learned to be patient and keep checking back. Dealers often get new stock, and persistence pays off. Over time, I managed to find some rare pieces that became highlights of my collection.

As the internet became more accessible, I started exploring online stamp dealers. The variety available online is astounding. Websites dedicated to stamp collecting, online auctions, and even social media groups offer endless opportunities to find stamps.

At first, buying stamps online felt risky. There were concerns about authenticity and quality. But by reading reviews and sticking to reputable sites, I learned to navigate the online market safely.

One tip I found helpful was to start small. I made a few small purchases from well-reviewed dealers to test the waters. As I gained confidence, I started bidding on auctions and even connecting with international sellers.

The convenience of shopping online and the ability to access stamps from all over the world without leaving home is unbeatable.

## Stamp Shows and Auctions

Stamp shows and auctions are two of the most exciting places to find stamps for your collection. Imagine walking into a large hall filled with tables covered in stamps from all over the world.

The buzz of excitement, the sight of rare stamps, and the chance to meet other collectors make stamps a must-visit event for any enthusiast.

At a stamp show, dealers set up booths to display their stamps. You can browse through countless albums and boxes, searching for that perfect addition to your collection.

Don't be shy about asking questions or negotiating prices. Dealers are usually happy to share their knowledge and might even give you a good deal if they see you're genuinely interested.

Auctions, on the other hand, offer a different kind of thrill. Here, you can bid on lots of stamps, often getting the chance to acquire rare and valuable pieces.

Before the auction starts, you can inspect the lots and make a list of the ones you want to bid on. It's important to set a budget and stick to it, as the excitement of bidding can sometimes lead to overspending.

One of the best things about attending stamp shows and auctions is the opportunity to meet fellow collectors. You can swap stories, share tips, and even trade stamps.

It's a great way to build friendships and expand your network within the stamp-collecting community. Plus, you might learn about other events and resources that can help you grow your collection.

If you're new to stamp shows and auctions, start with local events. These smaller gatherings can be less overwhelming and give you a chance to get comfortable with the process.

Once you gain some experience, you can explore larger national or international shows, which offer an even wider variety of stamps and opportunities.

Remember to bring a list of the stamps you're looking for, as well as a magnifying glass and a notebook to keep track of your finds. It's also a good idea to wear comfortable shoes and bring some snacks, as you might be walking around and browsing for hours.

## Trading with Fellow Collectors

Trading stamps with fellow collectors is one of the most exciting parts of stamp collecting. It's a great way to find new stamps, share knowledge, and build connections with people who share your passion.

I remember my first stamp trade vividly. I was at a local stamp show, nervously clutching a few duplicate stamps I hoped to trade. I spotted an older gentleman with a table full of beautiful stamps and decided to approach him.

We struck up a conversation, and I quickly realized how much I could learn from him. He patiently explained the value of the stamps I had and showed me some rare pieces from his collection.

We spent hours talking about our favorite stamps, sharing stories about how we acquired them, and discussing the intricacies of philately. By the end of the day, I had traded a few of my duplicates for some unique stamps I never thought I'd own.

Trading with other collectors is not just about the stamps; it's about the experience. You get to meet people from different walks of life, each with their own stories and collections.

These interactions often lead to lasting friendships and valuable connections in the stamp collecting community. Plus, you get to see stamps you might never encounter otherwise, broadening your knowledge and appreciation of the hobby.

One important tip for trading is to always be honest about the condition and value of your stamps. Transparency builds trust and ensures that both parties feel satisfied with the trade.

It's also helpful to do a little research beforehand to understand the approximate value of the stamps you want to trade. This way, you can negotiate confidently and fairly.

Another great way to find trading partners is by joining stamp clubs or online forums. These communities are filled with passionate collectors who are often eager to trade and share their knowledge.

I've found some of my best trading partners through online stamp forums. We exchange pictures and descriptions of our stamps, and sometimes even mail them to each other for inspection before finalizing a trade.

One memorable trade I made was with a collector from another country. We had been corresponding online for a while, sharing pictures of our collections and discussing our favorite stamps.

After several exchanges, we decided to trade. I sent him a set of rare local stamps, and he sent me a beautiful collection of stamps from his country. It felt like Christmas when his package arrived, and I carefully added those stamps to my album.

# Chapter 5: How to Evaluate and Identify Stamps

S tamp collecting is really fascinating. But did you know that it's not just about amassing a collection of pretty stamps? To truly succeed as a stamp collector, you need to be able to evaluate and identify the stamps you're collecting. Trust me, I learned this the hard way.

I remember going to a stamp collector's convention, browsing through the tables of various dealers. I came across a stamp that caught my eye - it was a rare, vintage stamp that I had been searching for for ages.

The dealer assured me that it was authentic and in excellent condition, so I happily gave him my cash and added the stamp to my collection.

Fast forward a few months, and I decided to sell the stamp to another collector who was offering a good price. But when I handed it over, he took one look at it and shook his head.

"This is a fake," he said. I was stunned. How could I have been so naive? Turns out, the dealer I bought it from was a scammer, and I had fallen for his tricks.

I realized then that I needed to learn how to properly evaluate and identify stamps if I wanted to avoid being scammed again. It's not enough to just collect them - you need to know their true value, their condition, and whether they're authentic or not.

This identification process is not as easy as it sounds as there are many factors to consider, from the paper type to the perforations to the watermarks.

It shouldn't be cause for alarm though. I'll relate my experiences and you should be able to learn how to spot a fake, how to grade the condition of a stamp, and how to determine its value.

At the end of the chapter, you should be able to confidently buy and sell stamps, knowing that you're getting a fair deal. And you'll never have to worry about being scammed again.

### Understanding Stamp Grading

Stamp grading might seem complicated at first, but it's pretty straightforward once you get the hang of it. Stamp grading simply means assessing the condition and quality of each stamp. The better the condition, the higher the grade, and the more valuable the stamp becomes.

When I started collecting, I had no idea what grading stamps meant. I remember buying a bunch of stamps from a flea market, thinking I had struck gold.

Later, I learned that most of them were in poor condition, with creases, tears, and faded colors. It was a bit of a letdown, but it taught me a valuable lesson about the importance of grading.

Stamps are usually graded on a scale from Poor to Superb. Poor stamps are damaged and barely recognizable, while Superb stamps look almost brand new, even if they're over a hundred years old. Most stamps you'll come across will fall somewhere in the middle, like Fine or Very Fine.

One of the first things to look for is the centering of the stamp design. A well-centered stamp has equal margins on all sides, which is highly desirable. If the design is off-center, the grade drops.

Perforations are another important factor. These are tiny holes around the edges of a stamp. They should be intact and evenly spaced. Torn or missing perforations can significantly lower a stamp's grade. I learned this the hard way with a rare stamp that had a few torn perforations. I had to accept that it wouldn't fetch a high price if I ever decided to sell it.

The condition of the gum on the back of the stamp is also crucial. Unused stamps with original gum are more valuable. If the gum is missing, disturbed, or heavily hinged, it affects the grade.

For example, a mint stamp from the early 1900s with a perfect front but disturbed gum can be still valuable but not as much as it could have been. Finally, watch out for any signs of damage, such as creases, tears, stains, or fading. Even the slightest defect can lower a stamp's grade.

Grading your stamps carefully ensures you understand their true value and helps you become a more knowledgeable and discerning collector. It's a skill that takes time to develop, but with practice, you'll get better at it and appreciate the finer details of your collection.

## Tools for Identification

When it comes to identifying stamps, having the right tools makes all the difference. Let me share some of my favorite tools and how they can make your stamp collecting journey much easier and more enjoyable.

First on the list is a good magnifying glass. This might seem obvious, but the level of detail on a stamp is incredible, and a magnifying glass lets you see those tiny features up close.

Whether it's spotting a small error or a unique marking, a magnifying glass is a must-have. I personally love the handheld ones with built-in lights – they make it so much easier to examine stamps without straining your eyes.

Another indispensable tool is a perforation gauge. Stamps are often identified by the number of perforations around their edges. A perforation gauge helps you measure these accurately. It's a simple plastic or metal card with a series of holes or slots.

You just line up the perforations on your stamp with the gauge, and voila! You can quickly determine the perforation count, which is crucial for proper identification.

Stamp tongs help you pick up and move stamps without damaging them. Using your fingers can transfer oils and dirt onto the stamps, which can ruin their condition over time. Stamp tongs have a smooth, flat tip that gently grips the stamps, keeping them safe and pristine.

A color guide is another handy tool. Stamps come in a rainbow of colors, and sometimes, the shade can be a key factor in identifying and valuing a stamp.

A color guide provides standardized color samples that you can compare with your stamps. This is especially useful for older stamps where the ink might have faded or changed over time. Matching colors accurately can help you avoid misidentifications.

Then there's the watermark detector. Watermarks are subtle patterns embedded in the paper of some stamps, and they can be tricky to see with the naked eye.

A watermark detector, often in the form of a fluid or special device, reveals these hidden marks. Knowing whether a stamp has a watermark and what type it is can significantly affect its value and classification.

Lastly, let's not forget about stamp catalogs. While not a physical tool, these catalogs are invaluable references. They list detailed information about stamps from around the world, including images, prices, and historical data.

Having a few good catalogs on hand is like having a personal stamp expert at your fingertips. They help you verify your findings and provide context for your collection.

Using these tools can make your stamp collecting journey so much more fun and efficient. They help you identify stamps accurately and also deepen your appreciation for the stamp collecting hobby. If you're serious about stamp collecting, investing in these tools is definitely worth it.

## Common Stamp Printing Techniques

Understanding the different printing techniques used in stamp production is essential for any collector. Each technique has its own unique characteristics that can help you identify and evaluate stamps more accurately. Let's dive into some of the most common methods and what makes them special.

First up, we have engraving or intaglio printing. This is one of the oldest and most detailed methods. The design is engraved onto a metal plate, and then ink is applied. When the paper is pressed against the plate, the ink transfers, creating a raised design. Engraved stamps often have rich textures and fine lines, making them easy to recognize.

Next is lithography which is a bit simpler. This method uses flat plates and relies on the principle that oil and water don't mix. The design is drawn with a greasy substance on a flat surface, and then the surface is wetted. When the ink is applied, it sticks only to the greasy parts, creating the image. Lithographed stamps usually have smooth surfaces and less detail compared to engraved stamps.

Gravure printing, or photogravure is another technique you'll come across. This method involves transferring a photographic image onto a plate with tiny cells that hold ink.

When paper is pressed against the plate, the ink from the cells transfers to the paper, creating the image. Gravure stamps often have a slightly blurry or dotty appearance, giving them a distinct look.

Then there's letterpress printing, also known as typography. In this method, the image is raised on the printing plate, much like a rubber stamp. The raised parts are inked and then pressed onto the paper. This technique was commonly used for early stamps and results in a slightly raised ink surface, which you can sometimes feel if you run your finger over it.

Screen printing or silkscreen printing is a versatile technique where ink is pressed through a screen with a stencil of the design. This method can produce vibrant colors and is often used for commemorative stamps. Stamps printed using this method usually have a flat, even ink distribution.

Lastly, let's talk about offset lithography. This is a more modern method where the image is first printed onto a rubber cylinder and then transferred to paper.

Offset printing allows for high-speed production and is commonly used for many contemporary stamps. Stamps produced this way have a smooth, even print without any raised or recessed areas.

## Spotting Fakes and Forgeries

One of the trickiest parts of stamp collecting is spotting fakes and forgeries. Believe me, I've been there. When I first started collecting, I was so excited to add a rare stamp to my collection that I didn't pay enough attention to its authenticity. It was a costly mistake, but a valuable learning experience. Now, I'm here to help you avoid the same pitfalls.

First, it's important to know that fakes and forgeries have been around for as long as stamps themselves. Some forgeries are so well done that even seasoned collectors can be fooled. But don't worry, there are several ways to protect yourself.

One of the simplest methods is to compare the suspect stamp with a known genuine example. Look closely at the details – the color, perforations, and design elements. If something looks off, trust your instincts.

Another tip is to use a magnifying glass or a loupe. This tool is essential for spotting tiny discrepancies that are hard to see with the naked eye. For example, genuine stamps often have fine, crisp details, while forgeries might look blurry or poorly printed. Check for any signs of tampering, like erased postmarks or added perforations. These are red flags that the stamp might not be genuine.

Watermark detection is another crucial technique. Many stamps have watermarks, which are subtle patterns in the paper that can help verify authenticity. To check for a watermark, place the stamp face down on a black tray and add a few drops of watermark fluid.

The fluid will make the watermark visible without damaging the stamp. If the watermark doesn't match what is expected, you might be dealing with a forgery.

I once bought a stamp that turned out to be a fake because I didn't know about watermarks at the time. I was so excited about the stamp's rarity that I skipped this essential step. When I finally checked, the watermark was completely different from what it should have been. It was a tough lesson, but it taught me the importance of thorough verification.

Certificates of authenticity can also be helpful. Reputable dealers and auction houses often provide these certificates for high-value stamps. They are issued by expert organizations and can give you peace of mind when making a purchase. If a seller refuses to provide a certificate or offers a dubious one, it's best to walk away.

Lastly, always buy from reputable sources. Whether you're purchasing online, at a stamp show, or from a dealer, make sure they have a good reputation. Look for reviews and ask fellow collectors for recommendations. Building relationships with trustworthy sellers can go a long way in ensuring you get genuine stamps.

Remember, spotting fakes and forgeries takes practice, but with these tips and a bit of vigilance, you'll become more confident in your ability to identify genuine stamps. And if you ever have doubts, don't hesitate to seek advice from more experienced collectors.

# Chapter 6: Organizing Your Collection

There's something truly special about collecting stamps. For many of us, it's not just about accumulating a bunch of pieces of paper with pretty pictures on them, but about preserving a piece of history, a piece of culture, or a piece of ourselves.

Whether you're a seasoned collector or just starting out, organizing your stamp collection is an essential part of the process. It's not just about keeping your stamps tidy and easy to find, but about honoring the time, effort, and passion that goes into building your collection.

When you first start collecting stamps, it can be overwhelming to look at the sheer number of stamps you've accumulated. But as you start to organize your collection, you'll begin to see the beauty in the process. You'll start to notice patterns, themes, and stories that emerge from your stamps.

You'll discover hidden gems and unexpected connections that you never knew existed. And as you continue to organize and curate your collection, you'll find that it becomes a reflection of your own personality, interests, and values.

Organizing your stamp collection is also important because it helps you to preserve the integrity of your stamps. When stamps are not properly stored or handled, they can become damaged, creased, or even lost.

By organizing your collection, you can ensure that your stamps are protected and preserved for generations to come. You'll be able to enjoy your collection for years to come and even pass it down to future generations.

So, whether you're a seasoned collector or just starting out, organizing your stamp collection is an essential part of the process. By taking the time to organize your stamps, you'll be able to appreciate the beauty and significance of your collection in a whole new way.

## Sorting and Categorizing Stamps

Sorting and categorizing your stamps can be one of the most enjoyable parts of collecting. The first thing you want to do is decide on a method for organizing your collection. Some collectors prefer to sort by country, others by theme, and some by the date of issue.

When I first started, I sorted my stamps by country. It helped me learn more about different places around the world, and it was fascinating to see how different countries designed their stamps.

One of the simplest ways to begin sorting is to spread your stamps out on a clean, flat surface. Take your time to look at each stamp and group them based on your chosen method. If you're sorting by country, make piles for each country.

If you're sorting by themes, like animals or historical events, make piles for each theme. This process can be time-consuming, but it's also very satisfying. I remember spending entire weekends just sorting stamps, completely lost in the process.

After you've sorted your stamps into groups, it's time to start categorizing them. This involves more detailed organization within each group. For example, if you have a pile of stamps from France, you might categorize them by year or by the type of stamp (commemorative vs. definitive). Using a stamp catalog can be incredibly helpful during this stage. A catalog will provide information about each stamp, such as its issue date, design details, and value.

One thing I found particularly helpful was creating a digital record of my collection. I took photos of each stamp and used a spreadsheet to log details like the country, year, and any special features. This not only made it easier to keep track of my collection but also helped me spot any gaps or duplicates. It was a bit of work to set up, but it made managing my collection much easier in the long run.

Personal experience plays a big role in how you organize your collection. When I started trading stamps with other collectors, I found it helpful to categorize my duplicates separately.

This made it easy to see what I had available for trade and helped me keep my main collection organized. One of my best trades happened because I had a well-organized list of duplicates that a fellow collector was interested in.

### Creating an Efficient Filing System

Organizing your stamp collection might seem like a daunting task, but it's actually quite enjoyable once you get the hang of it. When I first started collecting, my stamps were all over the place. I had no system, and finding a specific stamp was like searching for a needle in a haystack. Eventually, I realized that if I wanted to take my collection seriously, I needed a proper filing system.

The first step is to invest in quality materials. A good stamp album with clear pockets is essential. Avoid using materials that can damage your stamps over time. I once used an old photo album, thinking it would do the job, but I quickly learned that it wasn't acid-free, and it started to yellow my stamps. After that, I switched to albums specifically designed for stamps, which was a game-changer.

Labeling is another key aspect of an efficient filing system. I used small, removable labels to mark each section of my album. This way, I could easily see which country or theme each section belonged to.

Plus, it made it easy to rearrange and add new stamps without having to redo the entire setup. I remember the satisfaction I felt when I could quickly flip through my album and find the exact stamp I was looking for.

Digital tools can also be incredibly helpful. I started using a simple spreadsheet to keep track of my collection. I listed each stamp's details, such as the country, year, and any notable features. This not only helped me keep a digital record but also allowed me to quickly search for specific stamps.

One personal tip: Don't be afraid to experiment until you find what works best for you. I went through a few different systems before settling on one that felt right. At one point, I tried organizing by themes like animals, flowers, and historical events, but I found it got too complicated. Returning to a country-based system simplified things for me and made my collection more cohesive.

Lastly, regular maintenance is crucial. Every few months, I go through my collection to ensure everything is in order. I check for any signs of damage or misplacement. It's a good time to update my digital records and make sure everything is properly labeled. This regular upkeep keeps my collection in top shape and ensures that my filing system remains efficient.

Creating an efficient filing system for your stamp collection takes a bit of time and effort, but it's worth it. It not only makes your collection more enjoyable to browse through but also protects your stamps and makes it easier to find and appreciate them. Plus, there's a certain satisfaction in seeing your stamps neatly organized and knowing exactly where each one is.

## Digital Tools for Stamp Collection Management

Organizing your stamp collection can be a real game-changer, and thanks to modern technology, it's easier than ever. Gone are the days of manually cataloging each stamp with pen and paper. Today, there are plenty of digital tools designed specifically for stamp collectors that make managing your collection a breeze.

One of the first tools you might want to explore is stamp collection software. These programs are like a digital filing cabinet for your stamps. They allow you to input details about each stamp, including images, dates, and conditions.

This way, you can quickly search and sort through your collection without having to dig through physical albums. Plus, many of these programs have mobile apps, so you can manage your collection on the go.

Another great digital tool is online databases. Websites like Colnect and StampWorld offer extensive databases where you can look up information about virtually any stamp. These sites often provide details like the stamp's history, market value, and variations. This is super helpful when you come across a stamp you're not familiar with and want to learn more about it.

For those who love social connections, there are also online communities and forums for stamp collectors. Platforms like Stamp Community Forum and various Facebook groups allow you to connect with other collectors, ask questions, and share your finds. These communities can be incredibly supportive and are a great way to get advice from more experienced collectors or even discover new collecting opportunities.

Digital tools also make it easy to keep track of your collection's value. Many stamp collection apps and software have built-in features for tracking the market value of your stamps.

This can be particularly useful if you're considering selling some of your collection or just want to know how much it's worth. Some tools even offer valuation services where experts can appraise your stamps and provide a detailed report.

If you're looking to trade or sell stamps, digital marketplaces are a fantastic resource. Websites like eBay and Delcampe allow you to buy, sell, and trade stamps with collectors from all over the world. You can easily upload photos, set prices, and communicate with potential buyers or sellers. This opens up a whole new world of possibilities for expanding your collection.

Lastly, don't forget about digital storage solutions. Cloud services like Google Drive or Dropbox are perfect for backing up images and information about your stamps.

This way, you have a secure copy of your collection details that you can access from anywhere. It also provides peace of mind knowing that your data is safe in case something happens to your physical records.

## Labeling and Documentation

Labeling and documenting your stamp collection might sound tedious, but trust me, it's essential and can be fun! Imagine trying to find that one special stamp in a sea of hundreds. Proper labeling and documentation make it a breeze to locate and enjoy your favorite pieces.

Start by investing in some good-quality labels and a fine-tip pen. These will be your best friends as you label each section of your collection. When labeling, be specific. Instead of just writing "USA Stamps," break it down further, like "USA – 1950s Commemoratives." This way, everything is organized in neat, easy-to-find categories.

Documentation is where you'll keep detailed records of each stamp. A simple notebook or a digital spreadsheet can do wonders. For each stamp, note down its country of origin, year of issue, condition, and any special features. This not only helps in tracking what you have but also comes in handy if you ever decide to sell or trade your stamps.

Don't forget to add personal notes. If a stamp has a unique story or if you remember where or how you got it, jot it down. These little anecdotes make your collection personal and more enjoyable to look through. Plus, it's always fun to share these stories with fellow collectors.

Digital tools can also be a huge help. There are several apps and software designed specifically for stamp collectors. These can help you catalog your collection with photos, detailed descriptions, and even market values. Using these tools can save you time and keep your collection well-organized.

Regularly updating your documentation is key. Whenever you add a new stamp, take a few minutes to label and document it. This habit ensures your collection stays organized and up-to-date. It's much easier than trying to do it all at once later on.

Finally, remember that this process is part of the joy of stamp collecting. It's not just about the stamps themselves but also about the stories and the journey they represent. Taking the time to label and document properly will enhance your overall experience and appreciation of your collection.

# Chapter 7: How to Preserve and Maintain Your Stamps

As a stamp collector, you understand the importance of preserving and maintaining your valuable stamps. These tiny pieces of paper can hold significant historical and cultural value, and it's crucial to ensure they remain in good condition for future generations to appreciate.

Unfortunately, stamps are prone to damage and deterioration, which can result in significant loss or even destruction. This is why it's essential to take proactive steps to preserve and maintain your stamps.

Preserving and maintaining your stamps involves a combination of proper storage, handling, and conservation techniques. By taking the right steps, you can prevent damage from environmental factors such as light, humidity, and temperature fluctuations.

Additionally, you can protect your stamps from physical damage caused by handling, folding, or creasing. Proper preservation and maintenance can also help to prevent the growth of mold, mildew, and other contaminants that can damage your stamps.

There are several ways to preserve and maintain your stamps, and the method you choose will depend on the type and condition of your stamps. By following the right techniques and using the appropriate materials, you can ensure the long-term preservation and maintenance of your stamps.

This not only helps to protect their value but also allows you to enjoy them for years to come. Whether you're a seasoned collector or just starting out, it's essential to understand the importance of preserving and maintaining your stamps.

**Proper Storage Conditions**

Keeping your stamps in the best condition is all about how you store them. The first thing you need to know is that stamps are sensitive to their environment. They don't like too much light, heat, or humidity.

So, the best place to store them is in a cool, dry, and dark spot. Think of a closet or a drawer where the temperature stays pretty constant, and it's not too damp.

Now, about the light. Direct sunlight can be a real enemy to your stamps. It can fade the colors and make them look old and tired. Always store your stamps in albums or boxes that are opaque, so no light gets in. If you're displaying your stamps, make sure they're not in a spot where the sun hits them directly.

Humidity is another big deal. Too much moisture in the air can cause your stamps to stick together or develop mold, which can ruin them. Aim for a relative humidity level of around 50%. You can use a dehumidifier in the room where you store your stamps to keep the moisture levels down. If you live in a particularly humid area, this is especially important.

Temperature control is key too. Stamps like it cool, around 65-70 degrees Fahrenheit. Avoid storing them in places that get really hot or cold, like attics or basements. Sudden changes in temperature can cause the paper to expand and contract, which might damage the stamps.

It's also a good idea to store your stamps in albums with protective sleeves or in stock books. These are designed to keep stamps safe from dust, dirt, and physical damage. Make sure the materials you use are acid-free, as acids can cause stamps to yellow and deteriorate over time.

Handling your stamps with care is also part of good storage. Always wash your hands before touching them, or better yet, use stamp tongs.

This prevents oils and dirt from your fingers from getting on the stamps, which can cause stains and other damage.

## Cleaning and Repair Techniques

Taking care of your stamps is crucial to maintaining their value and appearance. When it comes to cleaning and repairing them, it's important to be gentle and use the right methods. Let's dive into some easy techniques you can use to keep your stamps in top shape.

First, let's talk about cleaning. Dust and dirt can accumulate on your stamps, especially if they've been in storage for a while. The best way to clean them is by using a soft brush, like a clean makeup brush or a small artist's brush. Gently brush off any dust or debris. Avoid using water or any cleaning solutions, as they can damage the paper and ink on the stamps.

If you come across a stamp with a smudge or stain, you might be tempted to try and remove it. However, it's important to be very careful. Most stains on stamps are permanent, and trying to remove them can cause more harm than good. If a stamp is really dirty or stained, it's often best to leave it as is rather than risk damaging it further.

When it comes to repairing stamps, less is more. Torn or damaged stamps can lose their value if not handled properly. If you have a stamp with a small tear, resist the urge to use tape or glue.

Instead, you can use a tiny amount of stamp hinge paper to gently hold the torn parts together. This won't repair the stamp completely but can help prevent further damage.

For stamps that are creased or bent, you can try flattening them out by placing them between the pages of a heavy book for a few days. Just be sure to put a clean piece of paper on either side of the stamp to protect it. This method works well for minor creases but may not completely remove deeper folds or bends.

Another handy tip is to store your stamps in a cool, dry place. Humidity and temperature fluctuations can cause stamps to curl, stick together, or get moldy. Also, consider using stamp mounts or stock books to keep your stamps flat and organized.

Lastly, always handle your stamps with clean, dry hands or use stamp tongs. Oils and dirt from your fingers can transfer onto the stamps, causing damage over time. Stamp tongs are specifically designed for handling stamps without causing harm. They're inexpensive and a great investment for any collector.

**Preventing Damage from Environmental Factors**

When it comes to stamp collecting, keeping your stamps in pristine condition is key. Environmental factors can wreak havoc on your collection if you're not careful. One of the biggest enemies of stamps is moisture.

Humidity can cause stamps to stick together, grow mold, or even discolor. To combat this, always store your stamps in a dry place. Consider using a dehumidifier in the room where you keep your collection, especially if you live in a humid climate.

Another threat to your stamps is direct sunlight. UV rays can fade the colors on your stamps over time, making them look dull and less valuable. To avoid this, store your albums and loose stamps in a shaded area.

If you have stamps displayed, use UV-protective glass in the frames. This way, you can enjoy showcasing your collection without worrying about sun damage.

Temperature fluctuations are also something to watch out for. Extreme temperatures, whether hot or cold, can cause your stamps to curl or crack. Try to keep your stamps in a room where the temperature stays fairly consistent. Avoid places like attics, basements, or garages, which can experience significant temperature changes.

Dust and dirt are common culprits that can damage your stamps as well. Keep your collection in a clean, dust-free environment. Regularly dust the area around your collection and consider using air purifiers to reduce the amount of dust in the air.

Pests, such as insects and rodents, can also pose a threat to your stamps. These critters might chew on the paper or leave behind unwanted residues. To protect your collection, store it in sealed containers or cabinets that pests can't easily access. Regularly check your storage area for any signs of pest activity and take action immediately if you spot any.

Lastly, always store your stamps in acid-free materials. Regular paper and plastic can contain acids that will slowly deteriorate your stamps over time. Use acid-free albums, sleeves, and mounting materials to ensure your stamps are protected. These materials are designed to be gentle on your stamps and prevent any chemical reactions that might cause damage.

### Long-term Preservation Strategies

When it comes to preserving your stamp collection for the long haul, there are a few key strategies you need to keep in mind. First and foremost, it's important to store your stamps in a cool, dry place. A climate-controlled environment is ideal, but if that's not possible, just make sure your stamps are kept away from direct sunlight and moisture.

Another important tip is to handle your stamps with care. Always use stamp tongs. Using protective storage solutions is also crucial. Stamp albums with acid-free pages are a great choice because they prevent the paper from yellowing and becoming brittle.

For particularly valuable or delicate stamps, consider using clear protective mounts. These mounts keep the stamps secure and protected from the elements while still allowing you to view and appreciate them.

Regularly checking on your collection is another good habit to get into. Every few months, take some time to inspect your stamps for any signs of damage or deterioration. Look out for things like mold spots, fading, or any new creases. Catching these issues early means you can take steps to fix them before they cause more serious damage.

If you notice any stamps that are starting to get damaged, it's best to address the problem right away. Sometimes, simply adjusting the storage conditions can help. Other times, you might need to consult a professional conservator, especially for very rare or valuable stamps. They can provide expert advice and services to restore and preserve your collection.

One often overlooked aspect of preservation is keeping a detailed inventory of your collection. Not only does this help you keep track of what you have, but it also provides important information about the condition and value of each stamp. Digital tools and apps can make this process easier and more efficient, ensuring that you have all the necessary details at your fingertips.

Finally, consider the future of your collection. If you plan to pass it on to family members or sell it eventually, make sure the next caretaker knows how to properly preserve and maintain it. Sharing your knowledge and passion for stamp collecting can help ensure that your collection remains in great shape for many years to come.

# Chapter 8: Specializing Your Collection

When it comes to collecting stamps, many people start out with a general interest in the hobby. They might collect stamps from different countries, or focus on specific themes like animals or landmarks. But as they delve deeper into the world of philately, they often find themselves drawn to a particular area that really speaks to them. This is where specialization comes in.

Specializing your stamp collection means focusing on a specific area of interest, such as a particular country, era, or theme. This can be a great way to deepen your knowledge and appreciation of the hobby, as well as make your collection more unique and valuable.

By concentrating on a specific area, you can develop a level of expertise that sets you apart from other collectors and makes your collection truly stand out.

Specializing can also be a great way to make your collection more manageable and enjoyable. When you're collecting stamps from all over the world, it can be overwhelming to try to keep track of everything.

But by focusing on a specific area, you can narrow your focus and really get to know the stamps and their history. This can make the hobby feel more intimate and rewarding, as you're able to explore the intricacies and nuances of your chosen area.

## Choosing a Specialty Area

Choosing a specialty area in stamp collecting is like picking a favorite ice cream flavor—there are so many delicious options, and each has its own unique appeal. When I first started collecting, I was overwhelmed by the sheer variety of stamps out there. It wasn't until I decided to focus on a specific area that my collection really started to take shape.

One of the first things to consider when choosing a specialty is what excites you the most. Are you fascinated by the history of a particular country? Do you love stamps with beautiful artwork or themes like animals, space, or famous people?

Think about what catches your eye and makes you want to learn more. For me, it was the allure of vintage airmail stamps. The idea of stamps that traveled across the world by plane was just too cool to resist.

Specializing doesn't mean you have to stick to one narrow category forever. It just gives your collection some direction and makes it more meaningful. You can always branch out later. For instance, after starting with airmail stamps, I expanded to collecting stamps related to early aviation and explorers. This kept things fresh and exciting, and I learned so much along the way.

Another great way to find your specialty is to think about your hobbies or interests outside of stamp collecting. Are you a history buff? Maybe you'll enjoy collecting stamps from a particular historical era or event. Love nature? Stamps featuring birds, flowers, or marine life could be your thing. Your personal interests can guide you toward a specialty that you'll truly enjoy.

You should also consider the availability of stamps in your chosen area. Some specialties, like stamps from certain countries or rare issues, might be harder to find and more expensive.

If you're just starting out, it might be easier and more affordable to focus on a more common area until you get the hang of things. Don't worry about starting small—every great collection begins somewhere.

Talking to other collectors can also help you decide on a specialty. Join a local stamp club or online forum and ask others about their specialties. You'll find that most collectors are eager to share their experiences and offer advice. Hearing about their passions might spark an idea for your own collection.

Lastly, remember that this is your collection, and the most important thing is that you enjoy it. Don't feel pressured to follow trends or collect what others think is valuable.

Choose a specialty that makes you happy, and dive in with enthusiasm. Your collection should reflect your personal interests and bring you joy every time you add a new stamp.

**Researching Your Focus**

When it comes to stamp collecting, finding a focus can make your collection even more enjoyable and meaningful. Researching your focus is all about diving deep into a specific area that interests you.

Whether it's stamps from a particular country, stamps featuring a specific theme, or stamps from a certain period, narrowing down your focus can be incredibly rewarding.

The first step in researching your focus is to think about what excites you. Do you have a particular country you love? Maybe you've always been fascinated by the history of the British Empire, or perhaps you have a soft spot for Japanese art.

If you're drawn to nature, you might want to collect stamps featuring animals, plants, or landscapes. The key is to choose something that you're genuinely interested in, so the research process feels more like a fun adventure rather than a chore.

Once you've chosen your focus, start gathering information. The internet is a treasure trove of resources for stamp collectors. Websites, online forums, and digital libraries can provide a wealth of information about your chosen area.

For example, if you're focusing on stamps from a specific country, you can find online catalogs and databases that list all the stamps issued by that country. These resources often include images, historical context, and other valuable details.

Don't overlook the power of books and magazines. There are countless books dedicated to various aspects of stamp collecting, many of which are written by experts in the field. Magazines and journals, such as "Linn's Stamp News" or "The American Philatelist," can also be excellent sources of information and inspiration. Your local library or bookstore may have a section on philately, so be sure to check it out.

Joining a stamp club or society can also be incredibly beneficial. These groups often have members with years of experience and a wealth of knowledge to share. They can provide insights and tips that you might not find in books or online.

Plus, being part of a community of like-minded individuals can make your collecting journey more enjoyable. You can attend meetings, participate in discussions, and even go on field trips to stamp shows or exhibitions.

## Building a Specialized Collection

Building a specialized stamp collection is like embarking on a treasure hunt. Instead of gathering random stamps, you focus on a specific theme or area that excites you.

This could be anything from stamps featuring birds, sports, historical events, or even stamps from a particular country. The joy of specialization is that it makes your collection unique and personal.

Starting with a specialization can feel overwhelming, but it's easier than you might think. First, pick a theme that you are passionate about. Maybe you love history, so you decide to collect stamps from different historical periods. Or perhaps you're a sports fan and want to collect stamps featuring famous athletes. Choosing something you genuinely enjoy will keep you motivated and make the hunt for new stamps even more fun.

Once you've chosen your theme, it's time to do some research. Look up which stamps fall into your chosen category and make a list. You can find information in stamp catalogs, online forums, and stamp collecting books. This research phase is like a detective mission, uncovering all the possible stamps that fit into your collection. It's exciting to see how many stamps relate to your interest and where they come from.

Next, set some goals for your collection. Do you want to collect stamps from a specific time period, or perhaps from different countries? Having goals helps you stay focused and gives you something to work towards. It can be as simple as wanting to collect all the stamps featuring butterflies from around the world or as specific as stamps from the 1960s space race.

As you start collecting, remember to document your finds. Keep a record of each stamp, noting where and when you got it, its condition, and any interesting facts. This will help you track your progress and see how your collection grows over time. Plus, it's always fun to look back and remember the story behind each stamp.

One of the best parts of specializing is connecting with other collectors who share your interests. Join stamp clubs or online groups where you can share your passion, trade stamps, and learn from others. Fellow collectors can offer valuable tips and might even help you find those rare stamps that are hard to come by.

## Showcasing Your Specialty

When it comes to showcasing your stamp collection, it's all about sharing your passion and hard work with others. Whether you're displaying your collection at a local stamp show or simply showing it off to friends and family, presenting it well can make all the difference. One of the first things you'll want to do is organize your stamps in a way that tells a story.

Think about what makes your collection unique and highlight those aspects. Maybe you have a collection of stamps from a particular country, or stamps that depict a certain theme like animals or historical events.

Creating a visually appealing display is key. Use high-quality albums or display cases that protect your stamps while allowing viewers

STAMP COLLECTING FOR BEGINNERS: FROM... 123

to appreciate their beauty. You might want to invest in stamp mounts or hinges to keep your stamps in place without damaging them.

Arrange your stamps neatly and in a logical order, perhaps chronologically or by theme. This helps viewers follow along and understand the significance of your collection.

Adding informative captions or notes can also enhance your display. These can be brief descriptions that explain the background of certain stamps, why they are important, or interesting facts about them. For instance, if you have a rare stamp, you might include a note about its history and how you acquired it. This not only educates viewers but also adds a personal touch, making your collection more engaging.

Don't forget to share your enthusiasm. People are naturally drawn to passionate speakers, and your enthusiasm can be contagious. Share stories about how you found certain stamps or what makes them special to you. This can make your collection more relatable and interesting to others.

If you're participating in a stamp show or exhibition, consider creating a theme for your display. A well-thought-out theme can make your collection stand out and catch the eye of judges and fellow collectors.

For example, if your collection focuses on stamps from World War II, you could design your display to reflect that era, using relevant colors and imagery. A cohesive theme ties everything together and creates a memorable experience for viewers.

Another great way to showcase your specialty is by getting involved in stamp clubs or online communities. These platforms allow you to share your collection with a wider audience and connect with other enthusiasts.

You can participate in discussions, share photos of your stamps, and even get feedback from more experienced collectors. This not only helps you improve your collection but also builds a network of friends who share your hobby.

Consider documenting your collection in a blog or social media account. Posting regular updates about new additions to your collection, interesting finds, and your experiences as a stamp collector can attract a following and encourage others to start their own collections.

Plus, it's a great way to keep a record of your journey and look back on how far you've come. Sharing your collection online makes it accessible to a global audience and can inspire collectors around the world.

# Chapter 9: The Art of Trading and Selling Stamps

A s a stamp collector, whether you're a seasoned enthusiast or just starting out, there comes a point where you'll need to trade and sell stamps. Whether it's to expand your collection, make room for new additions, or simply to make some extra cash, trading and selling stamps is an inevitable part of the hobby. But, it's crucial to approach this process with caution and knowledge, lest you fall prey to scams or overpay for stamps.

To truly succeed in trading and selling stamps, you need to be able to accurately assess the value of the stamps you're getting or selling. This means understanding the intricacies of stamp grading, condition, and rarity.

It's not just about the face value of the stamp; it's about the hidden secrets that can make or break its worth. Without this knowledge, you risk being taken advantage of by unscrupulous dealers or fellow collectors.

**Valuing Your Stamps**

Valuing your stamps can be one of the most exciting and, at times, daunting parts of stamp collecting. The value of a stamp can vary widely based on several factors, and understanding these can help you make informed decisions whether you're buying, selling, or trading. Let's break it down into easy steps so you can confidently assess the worth of your collection.

First, let's talk about condition. The condition of a stamp is a big deal. A stamp that's been kept in pristine condition, with no tears, creases, or fading, is generally worth more than one that's seen better days.

Stamps that still have their original gum (the adhesive on the back) are especially valuable. Think of it like buying a used book: a mint-conditioned copy will always fetch a higher price than one that's dog-eared and scribbled on.

Next is rarity. Simply put, the rarer a stamp, the more valuable it tends to be. Stamps that were printed in limited quantities, or those from countries with smaller postal histories, often carry higher values. This is where stamp catalogs come in handy.

Catalogs list stamps and their estimated values, giving you a good baseline to start from. Two popular catalogs are the Scott Catalogue and the Stanley Gibbons Catalogue. They can be your best friends when determining rarity.

Age can also play a role, but it's not always straightforward. Older stamps can be valuable, but not just because they're old. It's a mix of age and rarity. Some older stamps were printed in large quantities and are quite common, so they might not be worth much.

On the flip side, some modern stamps are incredibly valuable due to printing errors or limited production runs. It's the combination of age, rarity, and condition that you need to look at.

Don't forget about demand. A stamp might be rare and in perfect condition, but if no one wants it, it won't fetch a high price. Collectors' interests change over time. For example, stamps from certain historical events or with particular themes (like space exploration or famous artworks) might be in high demand. Keeping an eye on current collecting trends can help you understand which stamps are more sought after.

Another factor is provenance, which is a fancy term for the stamp's history. Stamps with interesting stories or those that were once part of famous collections can be more valuable.

If you have documentation or expert certification proving a stamp's authenticity and history, it can significantly boost its value. Think of it like having a signed copy of a book versus a regular edition.

Finally, consider the marketplace. Where you sell your stamps can impact their value. Selling directly to a dealer might be quick, but you might not get the highest price. Auctions can sometimes fetch better prices, especially for rare and valuable stamps, but they can also be unpredictable. Online marketplaces like eBay can be a good option, but make sure to research prices and be prepared for some competition.

Valuing stamps is a bit of an art, combining knowledge, research, and a bit of intuition. Over time, you'll get better at it, and soon, you'll be able to assess your stamps' worth with confidence. Remember, the goal is not just to find out how much your stamps are worth, but also to enjoy the journey of stamp collecting.

### The Art of Trading and Selling Stamps

Trading stamps can be an exciting part of stamp collecting. It's a great way to get new stamps and share duplicates. But it can also be tricky if you don't know what you're doing. So, let's dive into some strategies that can help you trade stamps successfully.

First, it's important to know the value of your stamps. You don't want to trade a rare stamp for something that's not worth much. Use stamp catalogs and online resources to find out the value of your stamps. This way, you can ensure that you're making fair trades. If both parties feel the trade is fair, it's more likely to be successful.

Communication is key in any trade. Be honest about the condition of your stamps. If a stamp has a tear or a missing corner, let the other person know. Misleading someone can damage your reputation in the stamp-collecting community. Plus, it's always better to build trust with other collectors.

Networking with other collectors can open up more trading opportunities. Join stamp clubs, online forums, and social media groups dedicated to stamp collecting. These platforms can help you find collectors with similar interests and increase your chances of making successful trades. Remember, the more people you know, the more trading possibilities you have.

Patience is another important strategy. Sometimes, you won't find the perfect trade right away. Don't rush into a trade just because you're eager to get a new stamp. Wait for the right opportunity where both parties benefit. It might take time, but it's worth it in the end.

Lastly, keep track of your trades. Make a note of what you traded, with whom, and when. This helps you stay organized and avoid any confusion later. Plus, it's nice to look back and see how your collection has grown through trading.

Trading stamps is a fantastic way to expand your collection and connect with other collectors. By knowing the value of your stamps, communicating clearly, networking, and being patient, you can make the most out of your trades. And who knows, you might just make a great friend along the way!

## Selling to Dealers vs. Auctions

When it comes to selling your stamps, you have two main options: selling to dealers or selling at auctions. Each method has its own pros and cons, and choosing the right one can make a big difference in how much you get for your stamps.

Selling to dealers is usually the quicker and easier option. Dealers are always on the lookout for new stock, so they're often willing to buy collections outright. You can find stamp dealers at shows, in specialized shops, or online. The biggest advantage here is convenience.

Dealers can give you an immediate offer, and if you accept, you'll get your money right away. But keep in mind, that dealers need to make a profit, so they might not offer you the highest price for your stamps.

On the other hand, auctions can sometimes bring in higher prices, especially for rare or high-value stamps. Auction houses will advertise your stamps to a wide audience of collectors who might be willing to pay more than a dealer would.

However, selling at an auction can take more time and involves some upfront costs, like listing fees and commission charges. You'll need to be patient, as it might take weeks or even months before your stamps go under the hammer.

Personally, I've had mixed experiences with both methods. A few years ago, I decided to sell a batch of my stamps to a dealer I met at a local stamp show. It was quick and easy; I got a fair price, and I walked away with cash in hand. But when I wanted to sell a particularly rare stamp, I opted for an auction. It was a longer process, but the stamp ended up selling for much more than any dealer had offered me.

One thing to remember when dealing with auctions is to choose a reputable auction house. Look for one with a good track record and positive reviews from other collectors. They should also specialize in stamps or collectibles. This can make a big difference in how well your stamps are presented and marketed to potential buyers.

Another tip is to set a reserve price if you're auctioning a valuable stamp. A reserve price is the minimum amount you're willing to accept. If the bidding doesn't reach this amount, the stamp won't be sold. This can protect you from underselling a valuable item, but keep in mind that setting a reserve that's too high might deter some bidders.

In the end, whether you choose to sell to dealers or through auctions depends on your priorities. If you need quick cash and want a hassle-free transaction, selling to a dealer might be the way to go. But if you're willing to wait and potentially get a higher price, auctions could be the better choice. It's all about finding what works best for you and your collection.

## Online Marketplaces

Navigating online marketplaces can feel a bit overwhelming at first, but once you get the hang of it, it's a fantastic way to expand your stamp collection. There are many platforms out there where you can buy, sell, and trade stamps with people from all over the world.

Sites like eBay, Delcampe, and HipStamp are popular among collectors. These sites offer a wide range of stamps, from common ones to rare treasures, and can be a goldmine if you know what to look for.

When I first started using online marketplaces, I was a bit hesitant. I wasn't sure how to spot a good deal or avoid scams. One of the best pieces of advice I received was to always check the seller's feedback.

On platforms like eBay, you can see reviews and ratings left by other buyers. This gives you an idea of how trustworthy the seller is. A high rating and positive reviews usually mean the seller is reliable.

One of my early experiences was finding a rare stamp I had been looking for on eBay. It was a beautiful, well-preserved piece that I couldn't find anywhere else. The seller had excellent feedback, and after a bit of research and comparing prices, I decided to go for it. The transaction went smoothly, and the stamp arrived in perfect condition. This experience gave me the confidence to keep exploring online marketplaces.

It's also important to pay attention to the details in the listings. Look at the photos carefully, read the descriptions, and don't hesitate to ask the seller questions. Most sellers are happy to provide more information or additional photos if needed.

This can help you avoid surprises and ensure you're getting exactly what you want. I once asked a seller about a stamp's condition, and they sent me close-up photos that revealed a small tear I hadn't noticed initially. It saved me from making a purchase I would have regretted.

Bidding on auctions can be thrilling, but it's easy to get caught up in the excitement and overspend. Set a budget for yourself and stick to it. Remember, there will always be other opportunities. I learned this the hard way when I got into a bidding war over a stamp and ended up paying much more than I intended. Now, I set a maximum bid in advance and avoid the temptation to go over it.

Another tip is to use the "watch" feature available on many platforms. This allows you to keep an eye on items you're interested in without committing to a purchase right away.

You can monitor the bidding activity and decide when the time is right to place your bid. This strategy has helped me snag some great deals by waiting until the last moment to bid, often catching other bidders off guard.

Finally, don't forget about the social aspect of online marketplaces. Many sites have forums and community sections where you can connect with other collectors. These can be valuable resources for advice, trading tips, and even finding rare stamps. Engaging with the community has not only helped me improve my collection but also made the whole experience more enjoyable.

# Chapter 10: Attend Stamp Shows and Exhibitions

A s a stamp collector, there's no better way to immerse yourself in the world of philately than by attending stamp shows and exhibitions. These events bring together collectors, dealers, and enthusiasts from all over the world, offering a unique opportunity to learn, network, and expand your collection.

I've had the pleasure of attending several stamp shows and exhibitions, and I can confidently say that they have been some of the most rewarding experiences in my collecting journey.

One of my most memorable experiences was at a stamp show in my hometown. I had been collecting stamps for a few years, but I had never really had the chance to meet other collectors or see such a vast array of stamps in person. The show was a revelation - I spent hours browsing through the various tables, marveling at the rare and unique stamps on display.

I even managed to pick up a few new additions to my collection, including a beautiful mint condition stamp from a country I had never seen before. The experience not only broadened my knowledge of stamps but also gave me a sense of belonging to a community of like-minded individuals.

However, as a newbie to stamp shows and exhibitions, there are a few things you should keep in mind. I'll relate my experiences so far and what I've learned from them.

### Preparing for Your First Show

Attending your first stamp show can be both exciting and a bit overwhelming. I remember the first time I walked into a large convention center filled with tables and displays. The sheer number of stamps, dealers, and collectors was staggering. But don't worry. With a bit of preparation, you'll be able to make the most out of the experience and enjoy every moment.

The first thing to do is to research the stamp show ahead of time. Most shows have websites where you can find information about the schedule, a list of exhibitors, and any special events or talks. Mark down the sessions or dealers you're particularly interested in. Having a plan will help you navigate the show more efficiently and ensure you don't miss out on anything important.

Before you go, make sure to bring along a few essential items. A small notebook and a pen are handy for jotting down notes or contact information. A magnifying glass can help you inspect stamps closely.

Don't forget a comfortable bag or backpack to carry any purchases and freebies. If you have a specific want list or a particular area of interest, bring a copy of it to show dealers.

It's also important to set a budget before you attend the show. With so many tempting items, it's easy to get carried away. Decide how much you're willing to spend and stick to it. Remember, there will always be another show and another opportunity to find that perfect stamp. Also, some dealers accept credit cards, but it's a good idea to have some cash on hand just in case.

One of my fondest memories from my first stamp show was meeting other collectors who shared my enthusiasm. I struck up a conversation with a gentleman who had been collecting for over 50 years. He shared stories about his rarest finds and gave me valuable advice on building my collection. Don't be shy—most people at these shows are happy to chat and share their knowledge.

**Hometowns honor their returning veterans, 1945**

Make sure to take breaks throughout the day. Stamp shows can be long and tiring, especially if you're on your feet the whole time. Find a spot to sit down, have a snack, and review what you've seen and bought so far. This will help you stay refreshed and focused.

## What to Expect at a Stamp Show

When you walk into a stamp show, you're stepping into a vibrant world where history, culture, and art come together. The first thing you'll notice is the buzz of excitement in the air. Collectors from all walks of life gather to buy, sell, and trade stamps. It's a friendly, welcoming environment where everyone shares a common passion.

As you move through the aisles, you'll see tables lined with albums, binders, and display cases. Each dealer has their own collection, offering a wide variety of stamps from different countries and eras.

It can be overwhelming at first, but that's part of the fun! Take your time to browse and explore. Don't be afraid to ask questions; dealers are usually happy to share their knowledge and stories behind their stamps.

One of the best parts of a stamp show is the chance to see rare and valuable stamps up close. Some dealers specialize in rare finds, and it's amazing to see stamps that you've only read about in catalogs. Exhibitions often feature displays of famous collections, showcasing historical pieces that tell incredible stories. These exhibits can inspire you and give you ideas for your own collection.

I remember my first stamp show vividly. I was a bit nervous, not knowing what to expect. But as soon as I walked in, I felt right at home.

I struck up a conversation with a dealer who had a fantastic collection of British colonial stamps.

He shared fascinating stories about the history of those stamps and even gave me tips on how to find similar ones. I left that show with not only new stamps but also a deeper appreciation for the hobby.

Another great aspect of stamp shows is the opportunity to network with other collectors. You'll meet people who share your interests and can offer advice, trade stamps, or simply chat about your collections. Many shows also have workshops and seminars where you can learn new techniques and expand your knowledge. These sessions are a great way to stay updated on the latest trends in stamp collecting.

Don't forget to bring a budget! It's easy to get carried away when you see so many amazing stamps. Plan ahead and decide how much you're willing to spend. It's also helpful to bring a list of stamps you're looking for. This can help you stay focused and make the most of your time at the show.

## Networking with Other Collectors

When you're into stamp collecting, going to stamp shows and exhibitions is like stepping into a treasure trove. But it's not just about finding cool stamps; it's also about meeting other collectors who share your passion. You might think, "Networking? Isn't that for business people?"

Nah, in the stamp world, it's more like making friends who geek out over the same stuff you do. You swap stories, trade stamps, and maybe even learn a thing or two from the veterans. It's like being part of a secret club where everyone's super excited about tiny pieces of paper.

At these shows, you'll bump into all sorts of collectors – from beginners like yourself to seasoned pros who've been doing this for ages. And let me tell you, talking to these veterans is like getting a crash course in stamp collecting.

They know all the ins and outs, from the rarest stamps to the best ways to preserve your collection. Plus, they're usually super friendly and eager to share their knowledge. So don't be shy; strike up a conversation and see where it leads!

One of the coolest things about networking at stamp shows is the chance to trade stamps with other collectors. It's like a giant game of show-and-tell, where you get to swap duplicates for ones you're missing in your collection. You never know what gems you might uncover in someone else's stash.

And hey, even if you don't find that elusive stamp you've been searching for, you'll still walk away with some new additions to your collection – and maybe a few new friends too!

But it's not just about trading stamps; it's also about building connections within the stamp community. You might meet someone who knows someone who has that rare stamp you've been coveting. Or maybe you'll find a mentor who can teach you the finer points of stamp collecting. The possibilities are endless when you start networking with other collectors. So don't be afraid to put yourself out there and make some new stamp buddies!

And let's not forget about the social aspect of stamp shows. Sure, you're there to buy, sell, and trade stamps, but you're also there to have a good time. Whether it's chatting with fellow collectors over a cup of coffee or attending a stamp-themed lecture, there's always something fun and interesting happening at these events. So why not take advantage of the opportunity to meet new people and expand your stamping circle?

## Showcasing Your Collection

One of the coolest ways to show off your collection is by hitting up stamp shows and exhibitions. These events are like treasure troves for stamp enthusiasts, and guess what? You can be part of the excitement by showcasing your own collection. Here's the lowdown on how to make your stamps steal the spotlight.

First things first, prep your collection. You want your stamps to look their absolute best, so give them a gentle clean and arrange them neatly. Next, decide how you want to display your stamps. Do you go for a classic album setup or get creative with a themed display? It's totally up to you! Just make sure whatever you choose, highlights the uniqueness of your collection.

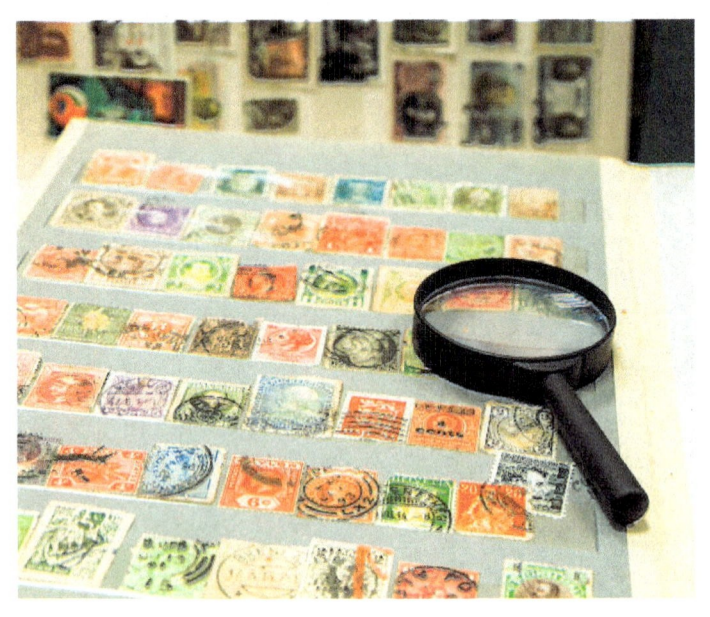

Now, onto the fun part – setting up your booth. Add some flair with colorful backdrops, informative posters, and maybe even a magnifying glass for those curious visitors. The goal is to make your booth inviting and intriguing, so people can't resist checking out your stamps.

During the exhibition, be ready to chat. Yup, you're the star of the show, so be prepared to answer questions and share cool stories about your stamps. Who knows, you might even inspire someone to start their own collection. And don't forget to network with other collectors – you never know what new gems you might discover.

# Chapter 11: Understanding Stamp Catalogs

As a stamp collector, you've probably heard the term "stamp catalog" thrown around, but do you really know what it means? In simple terms, a stamp catalog is a comprehensive guide that lists and describes stamps from around the world.

These catalogs are essential tools for stamp collectors, providing detailed information about each stamp, including its value, rarity, and condition. Whether you're a seasoned collector or just starting out, understanding stamp catalogs is crucial for building a valuable and meaningful collection.

For newbies, understanding stamp catalogs is especially important. Without a solid grasp of what stamps are out there and what they're worth, it's easy to get lost in the vast world of philately.

Stamp catalogs help you navigate this world by providing a clear and organized framework for understanding the stamps you're interested in. They also give you a sense of what's rare and what's common, helping you make informed decisions about which stamps to add to your collection.

But stamp catalogs aren't just for beginners. Even experienced collectors can benefit from using them to stay up-to-date on new issues, track changes in value, and verify the authenticity of their stamps.

With so many different catalogs available, it's essential to know which one to use and how to use it effectively.

## Major Stamp Catalogs and Their Uses

Stamp catalogs are a vital resource for any stamp collector. They offer detailed information about stamps from around the world, including images, descriptions, and values.

These catalogs can help you identify stamps in your collection, learn about their history, and understand their market value. Some of the most popular stamp catalogs include Scott, Stanley Gibbons, Michel, and Yvert et Tellier.

The Scott Catalog is probably the most well-known and widely used, especially in the United States. It's comprehensive, covering stamps from every country, and it's updated annually. I remember when I first started using the Scott Catalog; it felt like unlocking a treasure chest. Each page was filled with fascinating details about stamps I had never seen before. It became my go-to reference whenever I came across a new stamp.

Stanley Gibbons is another major player, particularly popular in the UK and among collectors of British Commonwealth stamps. Their catalogs are known for their detailed listings and historical information. Using the Stanley Gibbons catalog helped me better understand the stamps from British colonies, adding a rich layer of historical context to my collection.

For collectors in Europe, the Michel Catalog is a staple. Published in Germany, it offers extensive coverage of European stamps and is highly regarded for its accuracy and thoroughness.

Although the Michel Catalog is primarily in German, it's worth the effort to use it if you have a strong interest in European philately. I once used Michel to identify a mysterious German stamp I found at a local flea market. The sense of satisfaction was immense when I finally pinpointed its origin and value.

The Yvert et Tellier catalog, originating from France, is another excellent resource, particularly for French stamps and those from former French colonies. This catalog has a unique charm, with its elegant design and meticulous listings.

I recall using Yvert et Tellier to explore stamps from French Polynesia, a niche interest of mine. The catalog's detailed information made it much easier to navigate this specific area of collecting.

Using these catalogs not only helps you identify and value your stamps but also deepens your appreciation for the stories they tell. Each catalog has its strengths and can be a great tool depending on your focus as a collector. When I first started, I was overwhelmed by the sheer number of stamps out there. But these catalogs provided structure and guidance, making the vast world of philately more manageable and enjoyable.

Another personal tip: don't be afraid to mark up your catalogs. I highlight sections, make notes, and use sticky tabs to mark important pages.

These catalogs are meant to be used and loved, not kept pristine on a shelf. Over the years, my catalogs have become as much a part of my collection as the stamps themselves.

## How to Read and Use a Stamp Catalog

Stamp catalogs can seem intimidating at first, but they're invaluable tools for any stamp collector. When I first started, I was overwhelmed by the sheer amount of information in these catalogs. But once I learned how to navigate them, they became my best friends in the hobby.

When you open a catalog, you'll typically find an introduction that explains how to use it. This section is crucial because it details the catalog's layout, symbols, and terms. Spend a little time reading this part as it will save you a lot of confusion later.

I remember skipping this section initially, thinking I could figure it out as I went along. Big mistake! I ended up feeling lost and had to backtrack to understand the basics.

Next, you'll see the stamps listed by country and then by date of issue. Each stamp has a unique catalog number, a brief description, and sometimes additional information like color, perforation, and watermark details. Learning these specifics helps you accurately identify your stamps. One time, I misidentified a stamp because I overlooked a minor detail in the description. It taught me to pay close attention to every part of the listing.

Values are usually listed alongside the stamps. These values are a guideline for the stamp's worth in mint and used conditions. Keep in mind that these are just estimates and can vary based on the stamp's condition and market demand.

For example, I once found a stamp listed at $50 in the catalog, but I managed to sell it for $75 because it was in excellent condition and highly sought after.

Another important feature in catalogs is the use of symbols and abbreviations. These might indicate things like a stamp's rarity, whether it's part of a series, or if there are known errors. Familiarize yourself with these symbols. The first time I saw an abbreviation I didn't recognize, I ignored it, only to find out later it signified a rare variant of the stamp.

Don't be afraid to use multiple catalogs. Each catalog may offer slightly different information or values, and comparing them can give you a more comprehensive understanding.

I always cross-reference my findings with at least two catalogs to ensure accuracy. This habit has saved me from making costly mistakes and has even helped me spot valuable stamps that others might overlook.

## Finding Information on Rare Stamps

When you're on the hunt for rare stamps, knowing where to look and how to use the resources at your disposal is key. One of the most valuable tools for any stamp collector is the stamp catalog. These catalogs are filled with detailed information about stamps from all over the world. They help you identify stamps, understand their history, and assess their value.

A good stamp catalog will provide a wealth of information. You'll find details like the year of issue, country of origin, and sometimes even the number of stamps issued. This can give you a sense of how rare a stamp might be. For instance, stamps issued in limited quantities or those that were only in circulation for a short time tend to be more valuable.

Using a stamp catalog can be a bit overwhelming at first, but don't worry. Start by familiarizing yourself with the layout. Most catalogs are organized by country and then by the year of issue. Some even

STAMP COLLECTING FOR BEGINNERS: FROM...    163

have sections dedicated to specific themes or types of stamps. Once you know where to look, finding information becomes much easier.

One of the best parts of using a catalog is discovering the stories behind the stamps. I remember the first time I came across a rare stamp from British Guiana. The catalog described its history and how only a handful of these stamps existed. This added a whole new layer of appreciation for the stamp and made me even more determined to find it.

Here's a personal tip: don't just rely on one catalog. Different catalogs can offer different insights. For example, the Scott catalog might provide information that the Stanley Gibbons catalog doesn't, and vice versa. It's a good idea to cross-reference and see what each source says about the stamp you're researching.

## Cataloging Your Own Collection

Cataloging your stamp collection might sound like a daunting task, but trust me, it's a game-changer. When I first started collecting, I didn't bother cataloging my stamps. I had them scattered in different albums and boxes. It wasn't until I accidentally bought a duplicate of an expensive stamp that I realized I needed a system to keep track of what I had.

First off, get yourself a good stamp catalog. There are several well-known ones like Scott, Stanley Gibbons, and Michel and are valuable for identifying and valuing your stamps. Personally, I started with the Scott catalog because it's widely used and easy to understand.

Once you have your catalog, the next step is to create a system for your collection. I recommend starting with a simple spreadsheet. You can use software like Excel or Google Sheets.

List each stamp by its catalog number, description, condition, and any other details you find important. Don't forget to note the location of the stamp in your physical collection. This makes it so much easier to find a specific stamp when you need it.

When I began cataloging, I spent a few weekends just sorting through my collection. I made piles based on countries, and then smaller piles based on themes like animals, flowers, or historical figures. This helped me see what I had and what I was missing. It was a bit tiring at first, but I put on some music and made it a fun activity. By the end, not only was my collection organized, but I also rediscovered some beautiful stamps I had forgotten about.

One of the most rewarding parts of cataloging is seeing your collection grow and evolve. It's exciting to add a new stamp to your list and watch the gaps fill in. Plus, having a detailed catalog helps if you ever decide to trade or sell stamps. You'll have all the information you need at your fingertips, making transactions much smoother.

Don't be afraid to personalize your catalog. Add notes about where you found a stamp or any special memories associated with it. For example, I have a section in my catalog for "Travel Finds," where I list stamps I've picked up during my travels. Each entry includes a little note about the trip and why that particular stamp is meaningful to me. It adds a personal touch and makes my catalog more than just a list of stamps.

Finally, remember that cataloging is an ongoing process. As your collection grows, you'll need to update your catalog regularly. Set aside some time every month to review and update your records. This keeps everything current and prevents the backlog from becoming unmanageable. Trust me, staying on top of it makes the whole process much more enjoyable.

Cataloging your stamp collection might take some time and effort, but it's worth it. You'll have a well-organized collection that you can easily reference and enjoy. Plus, it gives you a deeper connection to your stamps, knowing each one's story and place in your collection.

# Chapter 12: Stamp Collecting as an Investment

Stamp collecting is a hobby that has been enjoyed by people of all ages for centuries. For many, it's a way to connect with history, explore different cultures, and simply enjoy the beauty of stamps. But did you know that stamp collecting can also be a means of investment?

Yes, you read that right - stamps can be a valuable investment, and with the right knowledge and strategy, you can move up the ladder from collecting stamps as a hobby to collecting stamps as a means of investment.

This is what makes stamp collecting even more exciting and rewarding. Not only do you get to enjoy the thrill of the hunt for rare and unique stamps, but you also have the potential to make a profit from your collection. Imagine being able to sell a stamp you've been holding onto for years for a handsome sum of money. It's a thrilling prospect and one that can make the hobby even more engaging and fulfilling.

However, before you start thinking of flipping and investing in stamps, there are a few things you should take note of.

## Assessing the Investment Potential

When it comes to investing in stamps, the first thing you need to know is that not all stamps are created equal. Some stamps are worth more than others, and their value can change over time. So, how do you figure out which stamps might be a good investment?

It starts with research. Look up stamps that have a history of increasing in value. Pay attention to stamps from significant historical events or those with printing errors, as they tend to be more valuable.

One of the best ways to understand the potential of a stamp is by looking at stamp catalogs. These catalogs list the values of thousands of stamps and are updated regularly. They give you an idea of how much a stamp is worth now and how much it might be worth in the future. It's like having a price guide that helps you make informed decisions.

It's also important to look at the condition of the stamp. Stamps in mint condition, meaning they are unused and have their original gum, are usually worth more. Stamps that are damaged or have been heavily used are often less valuable. This is where having the right tools and knowledge for proper preservation comes in handy.

Here's a personal story to illustrate the point. A few years ago, I came across a rare stamp from the 1800s at a local flea market. It was part of an old album someone was selling for just a few dollars. The stamp was in excellent condition and had a unique printing error.

I bought the album and later found out that this particular stamp was worth hundreds of dollars. It was a fantastic find and a great example of how being in the right place at the right time, combined with a bit of knowledge, can lead to valuable discoveries.

Another thing to consider is the rarity of the stamp. Stamps that were printed in limited quantities or have a unique feature are often more valuable. This is why it's crucial to educate yourself about different types of stamps and their histories. Joining stamp clubs or online forums can provide valuable insights from more experienced collectors.

Keep in mind that stamp investing is not a get-rich-quick scheme. It takes time, patience, and a genuine interest in philately. The market for stamps can be unpredictable, and values can fluctuate. However, if you approach it with the right mindset and knowledge, it can be a rewarding and profitable endeavor.

## Market Trends and Predictions

Stamp collecting has always been more than just a hobby; it's a window into history, a form of art, and for many, a smart investment. Over the years, the market for stamps has seen some interesting trends. Just like any other collectible market, it has its ups and downs, but certain stamps consistently hold their value, and some even appreciate significantly.

One trend I've noticed is the growing interest in stamps from emerging markets. Countries that are now experiencing economic growth often see an increase in the popularity and value of their historical stamps. For example, stamps from China have skyrocketed in value over the past decade. A few years back, I invested in some early Chinese stamps.

At the time, they were relatively affordable, but today, they've tripled in value. It's incredible how geopolitical and economic changes can impact the value of something as small as a stamp.

Another trend is the increasing demand for error stamps. These are stamps that were printed with mistakes, such as incorrect colors or missing elements. Collectors love these because they're rare and unique.

I remember finding an error stamp at a local flea market. It was a simple printing error, but because it was rare, it fetched a good price when I decided to sell it. It taught me that sometimes, imperfections can be more valuable than perfection.

Technology is also changing the stamp market. Online marketplaces like eBay and specialized auction sites have made it easier for collectors to buy and sell stamps. This has made the market more accessible, but it also means you have to be more careful.

There are more opportunities for scams and fake stamps, so always verify the authenticity of what you're buying. I've had a few close calls myself, but thorough research and using trusted platforms have kept me on the safe side.

Some countries are already experimenting with digital stamps, which could become a new area of interest for collectors. While it might seem strange to collect something that's not physically tangible, the uniqueness and traceability of digital stamps could make them highly valuable.

Personal experiences also shape our predictions about the market. For instance, I once bought a bulk lot of stamps from an estate sale. At first, it seemed like a mixed bag of common stamps, but hidden among them were a few rare gems that significantly increased the lot's value. This taught me that sometimes the best investments are found in unexpected places.

## Strategies for Building an Investment Collection

Building a stamp collection as an investment is a lot like putting together a puzzle. You need to have a strategy and a keen eye for valuable pieces.

One of the first things you should do is educate yourself about the market. Understanding which stamps are sought after and why they hold value is crucial. Start by reading books, joining forums, and following market trends. Knowledge is your best friend in this journey.

Another important strategy is to focus on quality over quantity. It's better to have a few high-quality stamps than a large number of common ones. Look for stamps that are in excellent condition. This means they should have no tears, creases, or stains, and their colors should be vibrant. A stamp's condition greatly affects its value. Always aim for the best quality you can afford.

One of my personal experiences highlights the importance of condition. I once bought a rare 19th-century stamp at a local auction. It had a small crease, which I thought wouldn't matter much. However, when I tried to sell it later, I found that the crease significantly reduced its value. It was a hard lesson, but it taught me to always check for flaws before making a purchase.

Diversifying your collection is another key strategy. Just like in financial investments, spreading your risks is a smart move. Don't put all your money into one type of stamp. Instead, consider collecting stamps from different countries, eras, or themes.

This way, if one area of the market dips, you still have other valuable stamps to rely on. A diverse collection is often more stable and can provide better returns over time.

Networking with other collectors and dealers is also essential. Attend stamp shows, join philatelic societies, and participate in online forums. These connections can provide you with valuable insights and access to rare finds. Sometimes, the best deals come from word-of-mouth rather than formal auctions or sales. Plus, building relationships with other collectors can make the hobby more enjoyable and rewarding.

A practical tip is to set a budget for your investments. Decide how much you're willing to spend each month or year on stamps. This helps you avoid overspending and keeps your investments within manageable limits.

Remember, while it's exciting to hunt for rare stamps, it's important to stay within your financial means. A well-planned budget will ensure that your hobby remains enjoyable and sustainable.

## Risks and Rewards

Stamp collecting as an investment can be incredibly exciting but also comes with its fair share of risks. It's like any other investment where you put your money into something with the hope that its value will increase over time.

But with stamps, you're dealing with a very specific market that can be unpredictable. Trends can change, and the value of stamps can fluctuate based on factors that are sometimes hard to predict.

One of the biggest risks is the potential for overpaying for stamps that don't appreciate in value. It's easy to get caught up in the thrill of acquiring a rare stamp and not do enough research on its true market value.

I've seen collectors spend a significant amount of money on stamps only to find out later that they aren't worth as much as they hoped. It's important to have a good understanding of the market and to consult with experts when making significant purchases.

Counterfeits are another major risk. The world of stamp collecting is unfortunately full of fakes and forgeries. It's crucial to be able to distinguish genuine stamps from counterfeit ones. This is where experience and knowledge come in handy, as well as getting certifications from reputable experts.

I once purchased what I thought was a rare stamp, only to later discover it was a very convincing forgery. That was a tough lesson, but it taught me the importance of due diligence.

However, the rewards can be substantial if you play your cards right. A well-curated collection of stamps can appreciate significantly in value over time. Rare stamps, especially those in excellent condition, can fetch impressive prices at auctions.

I remember selling a rare 19th-century stamp that I had found at a local flea market for a fraction of its actual value. After holding onto it for a few years, I sold it at an auction for a considerable profit. That moment was a testament to the potential rewards of stamp investing.

Another reward is the personal satisfaction and joy that comes from building a valuable collection. Each stamp has its own story and history, making the process of collecting and investing in stamps incredibly fulfilling. There's something special about owning a piece of history that can also grow in value over time. It's a blend of passion and smart investment strategy.

It's also worth mentioning the community aspect of stamp collecting. As you become more involved in the world of philately, you'll meet other collectors and investors who share your interests. This network can be invaluable for gaining insights, tips, and finding opportunities to buy and sell stamps. The relationships you build can greatly enhance your collecting experience and help mitigate some of the risks.

# Chapter 13: My Top Secrets for Finding Rare Stamps

As a seasoned stamp collector, I've spent years scouring for the rarest and most elusive stamps. And let me tell you, it's not always easy. But over the years, I've developed a keen eye and a deep understanding of what makes a stamp truly rare. In this chapter, I'm excited to share my top secrets for finding those elusive gems with you.

Now, I know what you're thinking - "Why would an expert like you share their secrets?" Well, the truth is, finding rare stamps isn't just about having a lot of money or connections. It's about knowing where to look, how to spot the hidden gems, and being willing to take calculated risks. And although it's not something most expert stamp collectors do, I'm willing to share my top secrets to help you find rare stamps too.

As someone who's been in the game for a while, I've learned that the key to finding rare stamps is to be persistent, patient, and always keep your eyes peeled.

It's not just about searching through stamp catalogs or attending high-end auctions. It's about being willing to dig deep, to explore the unknown, and to take the road less traveled. And trust me, it's worth it.

I'll be sharing my top secrets for finding rare stamps, from the best places to search to the most effective strategies for spotting those elusive gems. Whether you're a seasoned collector or just starting out, I hope you'll find these secrets helpful in your own quest for the rarest and most valuable stamps.

### Research Techniques for Rare Finds

Finding rare stamps can feel like a treasure hunt, and research is your best tool. One of the first steps I always recommend is diving into stamp catalogs. By familiarizing yourself with the most valuable and sought-after stamps, you can better recognize a gem when you see one.

Another essential research technique is online forums and collector groups. There are countless communities where collectors share their finds, tips, and knowledge.

Websites like Stamp Community Forum or even Reddit have active groups. I've learned so much from these communities, and they often have insights you won't find in books. It's also a great place to ask questions if you're unsure about a particular stamp.

Auction house archives are another goldmine of information. Many auction houses, like Spink or Cherrystone, have online archives of past sales. You can see which stamps have sold for high prices, how often certain stamps come up for sale and other valuable trends. It's a bit like studying the stock market but for stamps. By analyzing these patterns, you can make educated guesses about the future value of your finds.

Libraries and historical societies are often overlooked but invaluable resources. Many local libraries have extensive collections of stamp literature and periodicals. Historical societies can also provide context and stories behind certain stamps, adding a narrative to your collection.

For instance, I once found a rare stamp from the 19th century and traced its origins to a small post office in rural England through local historical records. That discovery made the stamp even more special to me.

Networking with other collectors can't be underestimated. I've often found that simply talking to other enthusiasts can lead to amazing discoveries. I remember attending a local stamp show where I struck up a conversation with a seasoned collector. He shared a tip about a lesser-known auction site where I eventually found a rare stamp at a fraction of its market value. It's these connections that often lead to the best finds.

Another secret is keeping an eye on estate sales and flea markets. These places can be hit or miss, but sometimes you get incredibly lucky. Finally, don't forget about online marketplaces like eBay. While you need to be cautious about fakes and overpricing, eBay can still be a great place to find rare stamps, especially if you know what you're looking for.

Setting up alerts for specific stamps or types can help you catch deals as soon as they're listed. I've found several rare stamps this way, and it's always exciting to snag a good deal right from the comfort of my home.

### Hidden Places to Search

Finding rare stamps isn't just about luck; it's about knowing where to look. Over the years, I've discovered some unexpected places that have yielded some of my best finds. These hidden gems can turn a casual collector into an expert with a keen eye for valuable stamps.

One of my favorite places to search for rare stamps is at estate sales. Many people overlook these events, thinking they're just selling old furniture and knick-knacks. However, I've found that older generations often had stamp collections that were tucked away and forgotten.

I remember one estate sale where I stumbled upon a box of old letters and envelopes. To my surprise, many of them had stamps from the early 1900s, including a few rare issues that were worth a significant amount.

Another great place to search is flea markets. These bustling markets are full of vendors selling a wide variety of items, often at bargain prices. It's a bit like treasure hunting; you never know what you'll find.

Antique shops can also be a goldmine for rare stamps. While these shops tend to focus on furniture and decor, many also carry small collectibles like stamps. The owners are often knowledgeable and can provide insights into the history of the stamps they sell. I have a favorite antique shop in a nearby town where I search for rare stamps. The owner always keeps an eye out for me and lets me know when new items come in.

Don't underestimate the power of online marketplaces either. Websites like eBay and specialized stamp collecting forums can offer a vast selection of stamps from around the world. The key is to know how to spot a good deal and avoid scams.

I spend a fair amount of time browsing these sites, and I've made some incredible purchases from sellers who were simply looking to clear out old collections.

Libraries and historical societies can be unconventional yet fruitful places to find rare stamps. These institutions sometimes receive donations from people who want to preserve their family histories.

While these stamps might not be for sale, you can often arrange to view and study them, and occasionally, they may offer duplicates for sale or trade. I've built relationships with a few local libraries and have been fortunate enough to acquire some unique pieces this way.

Another hidden gem is your own network of friends and family. Let people know about your interest in stamp collecting. You'd be surprised how many people have old stamp collections lying around, gathering dust in their attics or basements.

Lastly, don't forget to check out local garage sales and thrift stores. These places often have boxes of miscellaneous items where stamps can be hidden. It's a bit of a gamble, but the thrill of finding something valuable makes it worth the effort.

## Networking for Insider Information

One of the best ways to find rare stamps is through networking. You'd be surprised how much you can learn just by talking to other collectors. Attending local stamp club meetings, joining online forums, and participating in stamp shows opens you to a whole new world of information and opportunities.

Through these connections, you can learn various tips and tricks that will be invaluable to your collection. For example, one collector showed me how to properly clean and preserve delicate stamps, while another gave me insight into the best places to find hidden treasures. The knowledge shared within the community is endless and incredibly helpful.

One of my favorite ways to network is through online forums and social media groups. These platforms allow you to connect with collectors from all over the world, which means access to a wider range of stamps and information. I once joined a discussion about a rare stamp I had never heard of. The conversation led to a trade with a collector overseas, and I ended up adding a very unique piece to my collection.

Don't underestimate the value of attending stamp exhibitions and conferences. These events are not only great for seeing amazing collections but also for meeting industry experts and enthusiasts.

Another tip is to keep in touch with local stamp dealers. They often come across rare stamps and can give you a heads-up when something interesting comes in.

Building a good relationship with a dealer has helped me acquire several rare stamps that I wouldn't have found otherwise. They appreciate loyal customers and are usually willing to share insider information with you.

# Chapter 14: Advanced Collecting Techniques

A s a stamp collector, you've probably already mastered the basics of collecting and organizing your stamps. You know how to categorize them by country, era, and condition, and you've got a system in place for storing and displaying your collection. But now it's time to take your collecting to the next level.

## Plate Positioning and Varieties

Plate positioning might sound a bit technical, but it's one of those aspects of stamp collecting that can make your collection stand out. Simply put, plate positioning refers to the specific location where a stamp was printed on the printing plate.

Each stamp on a plate might have slight differences, making some positions more desirable or valuable than others. It's like finding a unique fingerprint within a sea of similar prints.

When you look at a sheet of stamps, you'll notice that each stamp isn't exactly identical to the next. This is because the printing plates can wear down over time, causing small variations. Collectors often seek out these differences, known as plate varieties, because they add a layer of uniqueness to the stamp. Imagine having a rare version of a popular stamp that only a few other collectors own. That's the thrill of plate varieties!

One of the most exciting parts of collecting plate positions is the hunt. You'll spend time examining sheets, looking for those subtle differences. It's like being a detective, spotting the tiny clues that others might miss.

For instance, a minor change in the design, a shift in color, or even a small flaw can indicate a different plate position. These variations can often be more valuable than regular stamps.

A great example of plate varieties is the famous "Penny Black," the world's first adhesive postage stamp. Collectors have identified numerous plate positions and varieties for this stamp, making it a fascinating and rewarding area to explore. Each variety tells a different part of the stamp's history and production process, adding depth to your collection.

Learning about plate positions also teaches you about the printing process itself. You'll understand how stamps were produced and the challenges faced by printers. This knowledge not only enhances your appreciation of stamps but also gives you a historical perspective. It's amazing to think about the craftsmanship and effort that went into creating each stamp.

If you're interested in diving deeper into plate positioning, there are plenty of resources available. Stamp catalogs, specialized books, and online forums are great places to start. You can also connect with other collectors who share your interest. They can offer tips, share their finds, and even help you identify unknown varieties in your collection.

STAMP COLLECTING FOR BEGINNERS: FROM... 199

So, the next time you come across a sheet of stamps, take a closer look. You might just discover a hidden gem that adds significant value to your collection. Plate positioning and varieties are what make stamp collecting endlessly fascinating, always offering something new to learn and explore.

## Perfins and Overprints

The word "perfin" comes from "perforated initials" or "perforated insignia." These are small holes punched into stamps to create a pattern, usually initials or a logo.

Perfins were originally used by businesses to prevent employees from stealing stamps for personal use. Think of them as an early form of security measure. When you see a stamp with tiny holes forming a pattern, you've got yourself a perfin.

Now, why would you want to collect perfins? Well, they're a fascinating part of stamp history and can be quite unique. Each business had its own perfin design, so they tell a story about the company and the era. Collecting perfins can also be a treasure hunt since some designs are rare and highly sought after by collectors. Plus, they add a layer of intrigue to your collection.

Overprints, however, are stamps with additional text or images printed on them after the original print run. These could be for a variety of reasons, like marking a change in postal rates, denoting a special event, or repurposing existing stamps for a new purpose. For example, countries might overprint stamps during war or political change to reflect new leadership or territory changes. This makes overprints a window into historical events.

Collecting overprints is exciting because each one has a story to tell. They can reflect political changes, economic shifts, or special commemorations. Plus, some overprints are quite rare, which adds to the thrill of the hunt.

One of my favorite things about perfins and overprints is that they challenge you to learn more. When you find a stamp with an unusual pattern of holes or unexpected text, it's a mystery waiting to be solved. You'll find yourself diving into research, learning about the history behind the stamp, and maybe even discovering something new. It's a great way to keep your collecting journey fresh and engaging.

If you're new to collecting perfins and overprints, start by looking for them in your existing collection or when you're buying new stamps.

You'll soon start to spot these unique features more easily. Joining a club or online forum can also be helpful, as experienced collectors often share their knowledge and tips. Trust me, once you start, you'll be hooked!

## Postal History and Covers

Postal history and covers open up a fascinating world within stamp collecting. Unlike collecting individual stamps, postal history involves studying the entire journey of a piece of mail—from the sender to the recipient. This aspect of philately can tell amazing stories about communication, transportation, and even social history. When I first dived into postal history, I was amazed by the layers of information a single envelope could reveal.

A cover, which is just another term for an envelope or package that has been mailed, often has stamps, postmarks, and addresses. Each of these elements provides valuable information. For example, postmarks can tell you where and when the item was sent. Sometimes, you can find special postmarks that commemorate events or places. It's like having a tiny piece of history in your hands, showing how people used to communicate.

One of my favorite covers in my collection is an old envelope from the early 1900s with a beautiful stamp and a clear postmark from Paris. It was addressed to someone in New York City. I found myself imagining the journey it took across the Atlantic Ocean.

This cover not only showed me a piece of postal history but also made me curious about the stories of the sender and the recipient. That curiosity is what makes collecting postal history so exciting.

Another interesting aspect of postal history is examining the different routes mail has taken over the years. Before the convenience of airmail, letters traveled by sea, often taking weeks or months to reach their destination. Some covers in my collection have fascinating stories of delayed journeys, rerouted paths, and even mail that was lost and found. These stories add a narrative dimension to the stamps and covers, making each piece unique.

Postal history also highlights changes in postal rates and regulations. By studying covers from different periods, you can see how the cost of sending mail has changed. Sometimes, you might come across covers with additional stamps added to meet a new postage rate. These details can offer insights into the economic and social conditions of the time.

One of the best parts about collecting covers and postal history is the thrill of the hunt. Finding a cover with a unique postmark or an interesting journey is incredibly satisfying. It's like being a detective, piecing together the story behind each item. I've spent countless hours at stamp shows and online auctions looking for those special pieces that add depth to my collection.

## Expertizing and Certification

Expertizing and certification can sound like intimidating words, but they are crucial parts of advanced stamp collecting. Essentially, expertizing is the process of having an expert verify that a stamp is genuine, while certification is the official document that proves this authenticity. For serious collectors, this process helps ensure that the stamps in their collection are real and often add to their value.

You might wonder why anyone would bother with this. Well, the world of stamps is full of fakes and forgeries, especially with rare and valuable stamps. Expertizing helps protect you from spending a lot of money on a stamp that isn't what it seems.

Getting a stamp expertized involves sending it to a reputable philatelic expert or a professional organization. These experts use various tools and techniques to examine the stamp's paper, ink, perforations, and other features. Sometimes, they even use ultraviolet light or microscopes to spot differences that aren't visible to the naked eye. The process can take a bit of time, but it's thorough.

Once the expert has examined your stamp, you'll receive a certificate of authenticity if the stamp is genuine. This certificate usually includes details about the stamp's condition and any unique features. It serves as proof that your stamp is real and can be very valuable if you ever decide to sell it.

You might be thinking, "Do I need to certify every stamp I own?" The answer is no. Certification is generally reserved for stamps that are rare, valuable, or particularly unique. For everyday stamps, it might not be worth the cost and effort. However, for those special pieces in your collection, certification can add significant value and credibility.

One thing to keep in mind is to choose a reliable expert or organization for the certification. Not all certifications are created equal. Some organizations have better reputations and are more trusted in the stamp collecting community. It's a good idea to do a little research and find a reputable expertizing service to ensure you get a valid certificate.

# Chapter 15: Future Trends in Stamp Collecting

Stamp collecting has come a long way since the days of the Penny Black. Over the years, this hobby has evolved and adapted to the changing times, and it's not showing any signs of slowing down.

As the world continues to evolve, we can expect to see some exciting new trends emerge in stamp collecting. For starters, the rise of digital technology has already had a significant impact on the hobby. Nowadays, collectors can access a wealth of information and resources online, from virtual stamp collections to online forums where they can connect with fellow enthusiasts.

But it's not just the digital space that's shaping the future of stamp collecting. We're also seeing a growing interest in more specialized and niche areas of the hobby.

For example, some collectors are focusing on collecting stamps that feature specific themes, like animals or famous historical figures. Others are drawn to the unique and quirky "Cinderella" stamps, which are stamps that aren't officially recognized by postal authorities.

And let's not forget about the impact of globalization. As the world becomes more interconnected, stamp collectors can access a wider range of stamps from all over the world. This has opened up new avenues for exploration and discovery, as collectors can now delve into the rich philatelic histories of countries they may have visited before.

So what does the future hold for stamp collecting? One thing's for sure – it's going to be an exciting ride.

## Digital and Virtual Collections

The world is changing rapidly, and stamp collecting is no exception. One of the most exciting trends in the hobby is the rise of digital and virtual collections. You might be wondering, what exactly does this mean? Simply put, it's about collecting stamps in a digital format rather than the traditional paper form.

First off, digital stamp collecting makes it easier to share your collection with others. You can showcase your prized stamps online without worrying about them getting damaged or lost. Platforms like online galleries and social media make it simple to connect with fellow collectors from around the world. You can easily swap stories, trade tips, and even exchange digital stamps.

One big advantage of digital collections is the ease of organization. Imagine never having to sift through piles of albums to find a specific stamp. With digital tools, you can categorize and search your collection with just a few clicks. Some apps even offer features like automatic identification and cataloging, which can save you a lot of time and effort.

Another great thing about digital stamp collecting is its accessibility. Not everyone has the space or resources to maintain a large physical collection. Digital collections allow anyone with a computer or smartphone to start collecting. This opens up the hobby to a broader audience, including younger generations who are more tech-savvy.

Security is also a major benefit. Digital stamps can be backed up to the cloud, ensuring that your collection is safe from physical damage like fire, theft, or loss. Plus, many platforms offer ways to verify the authenticity of digital stamps, reducing the risk of forgery or fraud.

Of course, some collectors might miss the tactile experience of handling physical stamps as there's a certain charm to holding a piece of history in your hands. However, digital and physical collections don't have to be mutually exclusive. Many collectors enjoy having both, appreciating the unique benefits of each.

## The Impact of Technology

Technology has transformed almost every aspect of our lives, and stamp collecting is no exception. Gone are the days when collectors had to rely solely on physical catalogs and snail mail to find and trade

# STAMP COLLECTING FOR BEGINNERS: FROM... 213

stamps. Now, with the advent of the internet and digital tools, the world of philately is more accessible and exciting than ever before.

One of the biggest changes brought by technology is the ease of finding and buying stamps online. Websites like eBay and specialized stamp auction sites have made it simple to browse, bid on, and purchase stamps from around the world. You can find rare stamps, compare prices, and even connect with sellers and other collectors with just a few clicks. This has opened up a whole new world of opportunities for collectors.

Social media platforms have also played a significant role in connecting stamp enthusiasts. Facebook groups, Instagram, and forums dedicated to stamp collecting allow collectors to share their finds, ask questions, and get advice from experienced philatelists. It's like having a global stamp club where you can interact with people who share your passion and learn from their experiences.

Digital tools have made organizing and managing collections much easier too. There are numerous apps and software available that allow collectors to catalog their stamps digitally. These tools often include features like image recognition, which can help identify and classify stamps, and cloud storage, so you can access your collection from anywhere. This not only saves time but also helps keep your collection well-organized and secure.

Technology has also enhanced the way we learn about stamps. Online resources, including digital libraries, educational websites, and video tutorials, provide a wealth of information at our fingertips. You can read up on the history of a particular stamp, watch a tutorial on how to properly preserve your collection, or even take virtual tours of famous stamp exhibitions. This makes it easier for beginners to get started and for experienced collectors to deepen their knowledge.

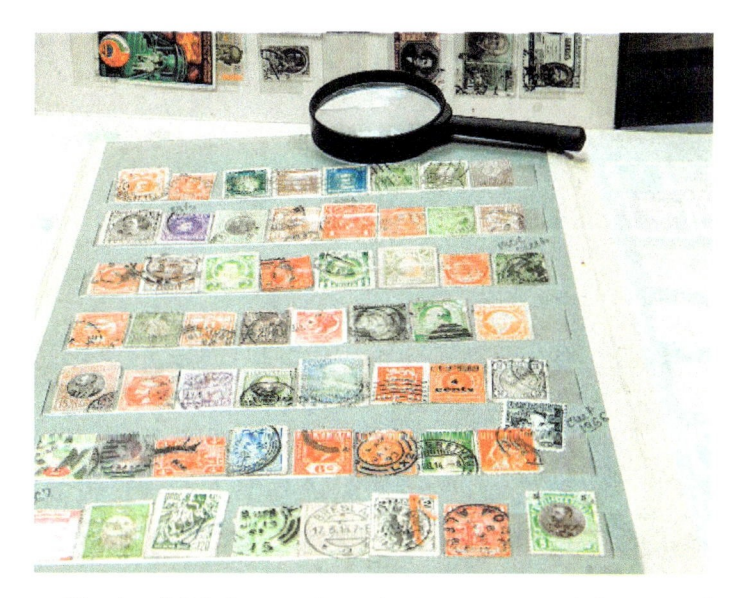

The rise of digital stamps is another interesting trend. Some postal services are now issuing digital stamps, which can be purchased and used online. While traditionalists might prefer physical stamps, digital stamps offer a new and innovative way to engage with philately. They can be collected, traded, and displayed in digital albums, adding a modern twist to the hobby.

Virtual stamp exhibitions and auctions have become more common, especially in recent years. These events allow collectors to participate from the comfort of their homes, breaking down geographical barriers and making it possible for more people to join in. You can view and bid on stamps in real-time, just as you would at a physical event, but without the need to travel.

Technology has made stamp collecting more dynamic and accessible. It has brought collectors closer together, provided new ways to buy, sell, and learn about stamps, and introduced innovative tools that make managing collections easier. While the core joy of discovering and collecting stamps remains the same, technology has certainly added new layers of convenience and excitement to the hobby.

## Emerging Markets and Interests

One of the most exciting trends is the rise of emerging markets in stamp collecting. Countries that were once off the radar for many collectors are now becoming hotspots for unique and valuable stamps. Places like India, China, and Brazil are gaining popularity, and their stamps are in high demand. These regions offer a fresh perspective and a treasure trove of stamps that many collectors in the Western world haven't explored yet.

Why are these markets emerging now? It's partly due to the economic growth in these countries. As people's incomes rise, they have more disposable income to spend on hobbies, including stamp collecting. Additionally, the global nature of the internet has made it easier for collectors to connect with sellers from all over the world. Online marketplaces and international shipping have opened up new opportunities to find and buy stamps from distant lands.

Another interesting trend is the growing interest in thematic collections. Instead of focusing on stamps from specific countries, more collectors are organizing their collections around themes. This could be anything from stamps featuring birds, sports, historical events, or even space exploration. Thematic collections are a fun way to bring together stamps from different parts of the world that share a common subject.

Technology is also playing a big role in shaping the future of stamp collecting. Digital tools and apps make it easier than ever to catalog and manage collections. Some apps can identify stamps using image recognition, provide market values, and even connect collectors with each other. These tools are making the hobby more accessible, especially for younger generations who are tech-savvy.

Speaking of younger generations, there's a noticeable push to get kids and teens interested in stamp collecting. Philatelic societies and clubs are creating programs and resources to engage younger audiences. They're using social media, interactive websites, and even gamified experiences to make stamp collecting appealing to a new generation. This is crucial for the future of the hobby, as it ensures that there will be new collectors to carry on the tradition.

Environmental and social themes are also becoming more prominent in stamp collecting. Many modern stamps feature designs that highlight important issues like climate change, wildlife conservation, and human rights. Collectors who are passionate about these topics are drawn to these stamps, and they use their collections to raise awareness and spark conversations.

Lastly, there's a growing interest in stamps from countries that no longer exist or have changed significantly over time. Collecting stamps from places like the former Soviet Union, East Germany, or colonial territories offers a fascinating glimpse into history. These stamps tell stories of political changes, cultural shifts, and historical events that shaped the world we live in today.

# Conclusion

Stamp collecting has taught me more than I ever imagined. It's not just about accumulating stamps; it's about the stories they tell. Each stamp holds a piece of history, a snippet of art, and a connection to a place or time. Over the years, I've learned patience, attention to detail, and the joy of discovery. The thrill of finding a rare stamp, the satisfaction of completing a series, and the friendships formed with fellow collectors are experiences I cherish deeply.

Looking ahead, I see my collection continuing to grow and evolve. There's always a new area to explore or a rare find waiting to be discovered. I plan to delve deeper into specific themes and perhaps even start new collections based on topics that pique my interest. Digital tools and online communities have opened up even more opportunities for expanding and sharing my collection, making the future of stamp collecting exciting and boundless.

To those just starting, welcome to an incredible journey. Stamp collecting can be as simple or as intricate as you make it. Don't worry about having the perfect collection right away. Start with what interests you, whether it's stamps from a particular country, era, or theme. Visit local stamp shows, join online forums, and connect with other collectors. Every stamp you add to your collection is a step forward in your journey.

One of the best parts of stamp collecting is the community. I've met so many wonderful people through this hobby, each with their own unique stories and collections. The camaraderie among collectors is special; we share tips, trade stamps, and celebrate each other's discoveries. It's a supportive and welcoming community that I'm proud to be a part of.

Even after years of collecting, I'm still learning. There's always something new to discover, whether it's a previously unknown stamp, a new collecting technique, or a fascinating piece of postal history. This constant learning keeps the hobby fresh and exciting. It's a reminder that stamp collecting is a lifelong journey.

One key lesson I've learned is to balance passion with patience. It can be tempting to rush and acquire as many stamps as possible, but the real joy comes from taking your time, appreciating each stamp, and building your collection thoughtfully. It's about quality, not quantity. Patience will often lead you to the most rewarding finds.

My final piece of advice is to enjoy the process. Stamp collecting should be a fun and rewarding experience. Don't get too caught up in the value of stamps or the pressure to find rare items. Instead, focus on the joy each stamp brings you and the stories you uncover along the way. Remember, every collector starts somewhere, and it's the journey that makes it all worthwhile.

I hope this book has provided you with the knowledge and inspiration to continue your stamp-collecting journey. Enjoy every moment, and happy collecting!

Printed in Great Britain
by Amazon